TOUR DU
MONT
BLANC

Vertebrate Publishing, Sheffield
www.**v-publishing**.co.uk

TOUR DU
MONT
BLANC

THE MOST ICONIC LONG-DISTANCE, CIRCULAR TRAIL IN THE ALPS

KINGSLEY JONES

TOUR DU MONT BLANC

The most iconic long-distance, circular trail
in the Alps with customised itinerary planning for
walkers, trekkers, fastpackers and trail runners

First published in 2020 by Vertebrate Publishing.

 **Vertebrate Publishing**
Omega Court, 352 Cemetery Road, Sheffield S11 8FT, United Kingdom.
www.v-publishing.co.uk

A CIP catalogue record for this book is available from the British Library.

ISBN 978-1-912560-72-1 (Paperback)
ISBN 978-1-912560-73-8 (Ebook)

Front cover: Traversing the Aiguilles Rouges towards La Flégère (Variation 9). © *Stephen Ross.*
Back cover: *Left:* Aiguille Noire de Peuterey viewed from Arp Vielle Inferiore (waypoint 51). © *Kingsley Jones.*
Right: On the ascent to the Bovine alpage (waypoint 121). © *Stephen Ross.*
All photography by Kingsley Jones and Stephen Ross unless otherwise credited.

Mapping contains Openstreetmap.org data © OpenStreetMap contributors, CC BY-SA.
Cartography by Richard Ross, Active Maps Ltd. **www.activemaps.co.uk**

 GR® is a trademark registered by the FFRandonnée. It designates the routes
identified under the name of GR® which are marked with white-red marks.
These routes are creations of the FFRandonnée and are reproduced here
under licence. For more information, please visit: **www.monGR.fr**

Design and production by Jane Beagley
www.v-publishing.co.uk

Printed and bound in Europe by Pulsio.

Vertebrate Publishing is committed to printing on paper from sustainable sources.

TOUR DU MONT BLANC
CONTENTS

TOUR DU MONT BLANC
INTRODUCTION

Tour du Mont Blanc (TMB)

Mont Blanc dominates the southern skyline as you fly into Geneva then, as you drive up the Autoroute Blanche to Chamonix, its stature grows. The magnificent brilliant white dome shines bright, high in the deep blue Alpine sky. It's no wonder that people travel from all over the world to trek the TMB, and what a unique experience it is, traversing 169 kilometres (105 miles) through France, Italy and Switzerland.

Each country has its own unique architecture and cuisine; there is a mixture of languages too. The geology changes, you see different flora and fauna, and the landscape evolves with markedly different aspects of Mont Blanc. The TMB rightly features on nearly every shortlist of the best treks in the world; it is unique in its mountain circumnavigation through three countries in such a relatively short trek.

There is no known date of a first completion of the TMB, but many sources cite Horace Bénédict de Saussure who walked around the entire Mont Blanc massif in 1767 while scouting out a route for the first ascent of the summit; the summit was eventually conquered by Jacques Balmat and Michel-Gabriel Paccard on 8 August 1786. The trails of the TMB predate Saussure's ramblings by a long way. There is historical evidence still visible of some sections of the TMB being used by the Roman military, though many of the trails were (and still are) shepherds' tracks between the villages and alpages.

Today tens of thousands of people traverse the TMB each year, and each season extra huts and gîtes open their doors to cater for the increased demand. The TMB is quite rightly such a popular route, and its unique attributes of circling the highest peak in the Alps, as well as traversing three different countries, are magnetic.

Acknowledgement

This book is dedicated to Sarah, my long-suffering wife, who has put up with my obsession with these trails and mountains for over twenty years, often accompanying me on them, and more recently introducing our daughter and dogs to them. Thank you!

About this guidebook

The TMB appeals to people who travel at all speeds, have different levels of experience in the mountains and of different ages; this guidebook is unique in that it caters for each category of user. You'll find other sources suggesting that you need to complete the TMB in a fixed amount of days, not allowing for the differences in the way people want to do the TMB. This guidebook has several unique advantages, making it indispensable and the most authoritative 'must have' guide to the TMB.

- Four user groups have been identified: **Walkers**, **Trekkers**, **Fastpackers** and **Trail runners**. Each of these user groups travel at a different speed, and typically have varied ascent and descent rates relative to their flat speed. The **Jones–Ross formula** has been devised, that modernises and develops Naismith's rule, to provide realistic timings for each user group between each timing point; see pages viii–xiii.
- The guidebook has been written exclusively for completing the TMB in an **anticlockwise** direction, as the vast majority of people do. The reasons for this are that there are no wasted pages of route directions that you won't use so the guidebook is lighter to carry; you are moving with the flow of people on the TMB so you see fewer people each day; and finally the sequence of ascents and descents are enjoyed in an anticlockwise direction both in terms of the terrain encountered and the views to be enjoyed.
- A companion map, the **Tour du Mont Blanc Guidemap**, has been produced to use in conjunction with this guidebook. Numbered timing points are shown on the map, along with accommodation and restaurants. This is to facilitate navigation, as generally a sheet map is easier to use and allows the wider landscape to be appreciated (and escape routes to be identified if necessary) rather than the mapping within a book which is necessarily constrained by the size of the book.
- **Points of interest** punctuate the book. You'll discover where to go wild swimming, learn about some of the famous faces in the history of the TMB, interesting features you'll pass, and top tips from where to stop for the best lunch to which are our favourite places to stay. These asides are golden local knowledge, and really enhance your TMB, rather than simply following a guidebook point to point.
- **Safety and planning points** feature heavily in this guidebook; this enables you to prepare for your TMB well and travel lightweight with minimal impact, but with the key safety gear. As well as keeping safe on the TMB, there's also a focus on how to ensure you can complete it, as well as to choose a realistic timescale and method, to ensure that you will enjoy it and to get the most out of your experience.

How to use this guidebook

To aid navigation we have split the route up into ***waypoints*** (numbered from 1 to 165, as well as additional waypoints on Variations 1–9); these are shown on the mapping and the route directions are split into waypoints. The waypoints are chosen to be an obvious point on the route (such as a bridge or a path junction). Some of the waypoints are also ***timing points*** (numbered from 1 to 34); these are spread along the route and enable you to plan your TMB before you go (booking your accommodation as necessary) because you will have a good idea of how long you will be moving for each day. The timing points are generally located at prominent points on the route where you might stop for food or accommodation (such as in villages or at mountain huts). This system allows readers to easily find where they are in the route directions and on the mapping.

We have identified four user groups for this guidebook. All user groups move at different speeds and have a higher flat speed than ascent and descent speeds, but they also move at different rates in ascent and descent.

Walkers move at a flat speed of around 5km/h and move at very similar speeds while descending and ascending.

Trekkers move at a flat speed of around 6km/h and move more quickly while descending than they do while ascending.

Fastpackers, who typically run on some sections of routes and walk on others, move at a flat speed of around 8km/h and move more quickly while descending than they do while ascending.

Trail runners move at a flat speed of around 10km/h and move far more quickly while descending than they do while ascending.

Personalised timings using the Jones–Ross formula

The modern Jones–Ross formula adapts Naismith's rule to calculate accurate timings on the TMB for the four user groups. *Table 1* shows how long each user group will take to travel between each timing point (TP). The last line of the table shows the total time it will take each user group to complete the TMB.

Bear in mind that the Jones–Ross formula applies for an average athlete, travelling at an average speed within their user group and carrying an average load. We have also made the following assumptions:

- normal conditions (without new snow, heavy rain or storms),
- no degradation in speeds over the days, due to fatigue.

In addition, the ascent and descent rates for each group could vary if you are, for example, a stronger ascender and weaker descender, or vice versa. As you follow the TMB you will quickly learn to adjust the Jones–Ross formula timings to fit your qualities of movement out on the trail.

SECTION				TIME PER SECTION (HOURS)			
Start	Finish	Distance (km)	Cumulative distance (km)	Walker	Trekker	Fastpacker	Trail runner
TP1	TP2	5.9	5.9	2:50	2:35	1:55	1:15
TP2	TP3	7.2	13.1	4:10	3:15	2:25	1:35
TP3	TP4	4.8	17.9	2:40	2:00	1:30	1:00
TP4	TP5	5.4	23.3	1:50	1:35	1:10	0:50
TP5	TP6	2.5	25.8	1:05	0:55	0:40	0:30
TP6	TP7	5.3	31.1	2:50	2:35	1:55	1:20
TP7	TP8	5.6	36.7	3:10	2:10	1:35	1:00
TP8	TP9	4.6	41.3	1:35	1:20	1:00	0:45
TP9	TP10	1.6	42.9	0:35	0:30	0:20	0:15
TP10	TP11	4.4	47.3	2:25	2:10	1:35	1:05
TP11	TP12	3.3	50.6	1:25	1:00	0:45	0:30
TP12	TP13	3.3	53.9	1:05	0:50	0:35	0:25
TP13	TP14	7.1	61.0	3:30	2:50	2:05	1:25
TP14	TP15	5.0	66.0	2:45	1:55	1:25	0:55
TP15	TP16	2.4	68.4	1:05	1:00	0:45	0:30
TP16	TP17	2.3	70.7	1:45	1:35	1:15	0:45
TP17	TP18	4.4	75.1	2:20	2:05	1:30	1:00
TP18	TP19	5.5	80.6	3:05	2:20	1:45	1:05
TP19	TP20	4.9	85.5	1:55	1:25	1:05	0:45
TP20	TP21	2.4	87.9	1:10	1:05	0:45	0:30
TP21	TP22	6.0	93.9	3:20	2:40	2:00	1:15
TP22	TP23	3.5	97.4	1:45	1:15	0:55	0:35
TP23	TP24	2.4	99.8	0:45	0:35	0:25	0:20
TP24	TP25	8.4	108.2	2:55	2:10	1:35	1:10
TP25	TP26	7.3	115.5	2:45	2:25	1:45	1:15
TP26	TP27	8.5	124.0	3:40	3:05	2:20	1:35
TP27	TP28	5.2	129.2	2:25	1:45	1:20	0:50
TP28	TP29	7.5	136.7	4:05	3:35	2:40	1:45
TP29	TP30	7.6	144.3	4:10	3:00	2:15	1:25
TP30	TP31	3.1	147.4	2:20	2:05	1:35	1:00
TP31	TP32	4.3	151.7	2:35	1:55	1:25	0:55
TP32	TP33	5.3	157.0	1:55	1:40	1:15	0:50
TP33	TP34	4.9	161.9	2:40	2:10	1:40	1:05
TP34	TP1	6.9	168.8	4:00	2:45	2:05	1:20
				82:35	66:15	49:15	32:45

TABLE **1**

SECTION				TIME PER SECTION (HOURS)			
Start	Finish	Distance (km)	Cumulative distance (km)	Walker	Trekker	Fastpacker	Trail runner
TP1	TP2	5.9	5.9	Day 1 7:00			
TP2	TP3	7.2	13.1		Day 1 7:50		
TP3	TP4	4.8	17.9			Day 1 7:40	
TP4	TP5	5.4	23.3	Day 2 8:25			Day 1 7:30
TP5	TP6	2.5	25.8				
TP6	TP7	5.3	31.1		Day 2 9:05		
TP7	TP8	5.6	36.7				
TP8	TP9	4.6	41.3				
TP9	TP10	1.6	42.9	Day 3 9:10		Day 2 7:45	
TP10	TP11	4.4	47.3				
TP11	TP12	3.3	50.6				
TP12	TP13	3.3	53.9		Day 3 8:45		
TP13	TP14	7.1	61.0	Day 4* 8:25			Day 2 8:40
TP14	TP15	5.0	66.0				
TP15	TP16	2.4	68.4			Day 3 8:45	
TP16	TP17	2.3	70.7				
TP17	TP18	4.4	75.1	Day 5 9:05	Day 4 9:30		
TP18	TP19	5.5	80.6				
TP19	TP20	4.9	85.5				
TP20	TP21	2.4	87.9				
TP21	TP22	6.0	93.9	Day 6 7:00		Day 4 8:30	
TP22	TP23	3.5	97.4		Day 5 9:05		
TP23	TP24	2.4	99.8				Day 3 8:15
TP24	TP25	8.4	108.2	Day 7 5:40			
TP25	TP26	7.3	115.5				
TP26	TP27	8.5	124.0				
TP27	TP28	5.2	129.2	Day 8 10:10	Day 6 8:25	Day 5 8:35	
TP28	TP29	7.5	136.7				
TP29	TP30	7.6	144.3				
TP30	TP31	3.1	147.4	Day 9 9:05	Day 7 7:00		
TP31	TP32	4.3	151.7				Day 4 8:20
TP32	TP33	5.3	157.0			Day 6 8:00	
TP33	TP34	4.9	161.9	Day 10 8:35	Day 8 6:35		
TP34	TP1	6.9	168.8				
				82:35	66:15	49:15	32:45

* End of day 4 (walker): there is no accommodation at TP16; either stop in Courmayeur (between TP15 and TP16) or stop at Rifugio Bertone (just before TP17).

TABLE **2**

Looking towards Col de la Seigne from Lago Combal (waypoint 50). © *Kingsley Jones*.

Planning your TMB using the Jones–Ross formula

To plan your route:
- decide which user group you fit into,
- decide how long you want to be on the move for each day,
- look at the timings in *Table 1* to work out how to split your TMB up,
- refer to the accommodation directory (pages 108–117) to plan where to stay each night.

Table 2 (opposite) shows an example itinerary for each user group. Each coloured box denotes a day on the TMB, with the time spent on the move each day shown in the appropriate box. In this example walkers finish the TMB in ten days, trekkers in eight days, fastpackers in six days and trail runners in four days. Most days in our example are around eight or nine hours, with occasional shorter or longer days. Obviously you can design your own itinerary to suit your own needs.

Route variations

One of the assets of the TMB is the wide variety of route variations available, but it can be difficult to decide which ones to use. In the route directions you will find information about what each variation is like, and the advantages and disadvantages of using it compared to the main route. You will also need to know how long the variations will take, when compared with the same section of the main route. *Table 3* shows the route variations, their start and finish points, and how long each user group will take to complete them; it also shows the equivalent figures for the corresponding section of the main route.

	SECTION			TIME PER SECTION (HOURS)			
	Start	Finish	Distance (km)	Walker	Trekker	Fastpacker	Trail runner
Variation 1	TP2	TP4	10.8	04:30	03:25	02:35	01:45
Equivalent section of main route	TP2	TP4	12.0	06:50	05:15	03:55	02:35
Variation 2	TP7	TP9	5.5	03:25	02:25	01:50	01:10
Equivalent section of main route	TP7	TP9	10.2	04:45	03:30	02:35	01:45
Variation 3	TP16	TP18	5.2	03:25	03:05	02:20	01:30
Equivalent section of main route	TP16	TP18	6.7	04:05	03:40	02:45	01:45
Variation 4	TP17	TP19	7.4	02:35	02:05	01:35	01:05
Equivalent section of main route	TP17	TP19	9.9	05:25	04:25	03:15	02:05
Variation 5	TP26	TP28	12.6	07:40	06:05	04:35	02:55
Equivalent section of main route	TP26	TP28	13.7	06:05	04:50	03:40	02:25
Variation 6	TP28	TP29	8.9	03:45	03:15	02:25	01:40
Equivalent section of main route	TP28	TP29	7.5	04:05	03:35	02:40	01:45
Variation 7	TP29	TP30	6.2	03:10	02:15	01:40	01:05
Equivalent section of main route	TP29	TP30	7.6	04:10	03:00	02:15	01:25
Variation 8	TP30	TP31	4.2	02:35	02:20	01:45	01:10
Equivalent section of main route	TP30	TP31	3.1	02:20	02:05	01:35	01:00
Variation 9	TP31	TP32	3.3	01:25	01:00	00:45	00:30
Equivalent section of main route	TP31	TP32	4.3	02:35	01:55	01:25	00:55

TABLE **3**

As you will see from the map, it is possible to do Variation 5 then join Variation 6 part way along it (this is fully explained in the route description – see page 81); if you decide to do this you can take a bit of time off the combined time for Variations 5 and 6 to provide a reasonable estimate of how long it will take.

The Jones–Ross formula in detail

Expressed in words, the Jones–Ross formula is:

$$\text{time} = \frac{\text{distance}}{\text{flat speed}} + \text{adjustment for ascent} + \text{adjustment for descent}$$

More precisely, it can be expressed as:

$$\frac{\text{time}}{\text{(minutes)}} = \frac{\text{distance (km)}}{\text{flat speed (km per hour)}/60} + \frac{\text{vertical ascent (metres)}}{\text{vertical ascent speed (metres per hour)}/60} + \frac{\text{vertical descent (metres)}}{\text{vertical descent speed (metres per hour)}/60}$$

The flat speeds and vertical ascent and descent speeds for the four user groups are shown in *Table 4*.

	Flat speed (km per hour)	Vertical ascent speed (metres ascended per hour)	Vertical descent speed (metres descended per hour)
Walker	5	425	450
Trekker	6	450	750
Fastpacker	8	600	1000
Trail runner	10	1000	2000

TABLE **4**

Transport

Geneva is the closest international city to the TMB. TGV high-speed trains, direct from Paris to Geneva, take approximately three hours and run up to once every two hours. Good connections can be made to other French stations, Brussels, Amsterdam, and Germany and to London via the Eurostar. Direct trains connect Paris to Saint-Gervais-les-Bains–Le Fayet and Chamonix, but are much slower and infrequent.

The nearest airport to the TMB is Geneva Airport; if possible you should select flights that arrive in the Swiss Sector (rather than the French Sector), as that is where all the buses and transfer shuttles you will need depart from. A local train shuttle connects the airport to the city centre, running approximately three times an hour.

The main location to head to for the start of the TMB is Chamonix, near the official start at Les Houches, in France. To get to the TMB from Geneva by train, take the Léman Express train line from the city centre to Saint-Gervais-les-Bains–Le Fayet, then take the Mont Blanc Express regional train line to Chamonix. The Mont Blanc Express also connects Martigny in Switzerland to Chamonix. Chamonix is the best served point by transfers from Geneva Airport; many companies ply this route several times a day; see page 107. Local buses and trains are available between Chamonix and Les Houches.

For those considering splitting the TMB into two weekends as a fastpacker (six days in total) or a trail runner (four days in total), you'll need to travel from Courmayeur, Italy, at the end of the first weekend and get back to Courmayeur

Worked example

For the first leg of the TMB, we need the following figures:

Start: TP1
Finish: TP2
Distance: 5.9 kilometres
Ascent: 684 metres
Descent: 34 metres

For a walker

$$\text{time} = \frac{5.9}{5/60} + \frac{684}{425/60} + \frac{34}{450/60} = 171.9 \text{ minutes}$$

For a trail runner

$$\text{time} = \frac{5.9}{10/60} + \frac{684}{1000/60} + \frac{34}{2000/60} = 77.5 \text{ minutes}$$

The Aiguillette d'Argentière (waypoint 139). © *Stephen Ross*.

at the start of the second weekend. To get to Courmayeur from France or Switzerland, the easiest method is to travel to Chamonix then catch the regular SAVDA or SAT bus that transports you through the Mont Blanc road tunnel to Courmayeur. There are generally six departures a day during the summer season.

Seasonal weather and when to go

If you plan to stay in mountain huts, gîtes and lodges along the trail, the majority are open from mid-June until mid-September. They are businesses, and if they realistically thought that there was a longer guaranteed season to be open, they would be. It's not to say that the TMB can't be hiked outside the season in some years, but generally there is too much snow earlier in the year for it to be safe, and the weather often deteriorates later in the year.

Once the TMB accommodation is closed for the season, the infrastructure that is dependent on the TMB closes too. Valley buses switch to low-season schedules, shops close until the winter season starts, and even water troughs are turned off. An out-of-season TMB requires a far greater level of autonomy, carrying bigger loads, a lesser degree of safety without the mountain hut network as well as requiring winter mountaineering skills and equipment, so unless you are content with these factors, it is not recommended.

People always question when the best time is to do the TMB. Here is how the seasons usually work out.

Early season: mid-June to early July

There is still quite a lot of old spring snow on the ground, which necessitates the crossing of several snow slopes where a slip would be serious. Having said this, it is generally stable weather and a relatively quiet time of year.

High season: early July to end of July

A high pressure anticyclone usually dominates over the Alps in this period, with long sunny days that soon melt back the snow patches. The streams are at their meltwater maximum, and snow bridges need to be crossed carefully.

Peak season: August

The good weather usually continues, and coincides with most European summer holidays, so the trails are busy, and the accommodation gets booked up early. Late afternoon convection storms, that dissipate the humidity, are common. The last weekend in August sees the Ultra-Trail du Mont Blanc (UTMB) trail running race, with nearly 10,000 runners on the TMB trails. Be aware when this event is on!

High season: first ten days of September

When the dust has settled after the UTMB, early September is always busy with people choosing to do the TMB straight after schools have returned for the autumn term. Many others have the same cunning plan, so this is a busy period.

Late season: middle ten days of September

These are the last days of the season on the TMB and are often the choice of the cognoscenti. Just before the mountain huts close, the weather is generally slightly cooler, and the days start to draw in, but the trails can be lovely and quiet.

Safety and mountain rescue

You should always carry a mobile phone on the TMB in order to alert mountain rescue in the event of an accident. There is generally good mobile phone signal on the route, apart from in the steep-sided Les Chapieux valley between Col du Bonhomme and Col de la Seigne (waypoints 30–45). All mountain huts and most farms in the region have landlines. Also, any guided groups you see led by UIMLA members should have a rescue radio or satellite phone. There isn't anywhere on the TMB where you are more than thirty to sixty minutes from a landline or mobile phone signal.

Before you start the TMB, you should save the following emergency and mountain rescue numbers into your mobile phone, so they are immediately available in the event of an accident.

Emergency services
France – 112
Italy – 112 or 118
Switzerland – 144.

Mountain rescue
France – PGHM Chamonix, +33 (0)4 50 53 16 89
France – PGHM Bourg St Maurice, +33 (0)4 79 07 01 10
Italy – Val d'Aosta, +39 (0)165 238 222
Switzerland – REGA 1414.

In the event of needing to call mountain rescue, you should prepare the following information that will be asked of you.

- *Your name* – normally you are asked your full name, and sometimes even your address, to identify you. Your mobile number will show on the emergency operator's screen, but you may be asked to confirm it.
- *Where you are* – make sure you know how to locate your UTM coordinates using your mobile phone or smartwatch. In France the PGHM (Peloton de Gendarmerie de Haute Montagne) use GendLoc (similar to SARLOC in the UK) to send you a text message to enable your mobile phone to send them your position. The maps in this guidebook have nearby named positions that will help to identify your position, allied with altitude data from the map or your mobile phone or GPS device.
- *Phone number* – if you are low on battery, tell the operator and provide an alternative phone number of another group member who has good battery strength and signal.
- *What occurred* – detail the event that occurred in terms of numbers involved, their ages and injuries sustained. You will also be asked how these were sustained, such as a fall or sudden illness. Provide any detail you feel pertinent, such as fractures, medication or the time elapsed since the accident.
- *Rescuer details* – you may be asked various details that the helicopter crew might require, such as estimated wind speed, cloud base, visibility and prevailing conditions.

Try and remain calm when providing this information, as your clarity and quality of the information is of vital importance to the rescue team. It is well worth practising this phone call as part of your pre-trip training, so that all team members are aware of what may be asked of them too.

When a rescue helicopter arrives, the air crew will decide on a suitable location to land or winch someone down to you. Crouch down and secure all loose items that could get sucked into the helicopter engines. Wear eye protection such as sunglasses to protect your eyes from debris from the downdraught. If you have

TMB signs showing the way through the cobbled streets of Dolonne (waypoint 65). © *Kingsley Jones.*

the option to signal to the helicopter, raise two arms above your head in a Y shape to indicate you require rescue. Where you know the wind direction, it is useful to the pilot for you to stand with your back to the wind, where practicable. Do not attempt to approach the helicopter; wait for instructions from the crew before you do anything.

As in the UK or your home country, mountain rescue is there as a last resort. Whether professional or volunteer, it is staffed by men and women just like you, who all have homes, friends and families to return to. Genuine accidents do happen, and no rescue team resents a call out for one second for that, but helicopters are not taxis if you are tired or lost. Respect them, and they will be there in your hour of need.

Distress signal
In the Alps the distress signal is six blasts of a whistle evenly spaced over one minute, followed by a break of one minute. Then repeat. The response that confirms that your signal has been received is three blasts of a whistle over one minute followed by a break of one minute. At night, flashes of a torch in the same sequence can be used instead. Always carry a torch and a whistle.

Need help?
Body language when signalling an approaching helicopter from the ground:

*Make a 'Y' with
your arms to signal*
YES – I need help

*Make an 'N' with
your arms to signal*
NO – Help is not needed

When signalling, stay still, and remain in your signalling position.

Insurance and emergencies

Unlike areas such as the UK, where mountain rescue is provided by volunteers, supported by the HM Coastguard and various air ambulances, mountain rescue services in the Alps are mainly helicopter based and operated by full-time professionals. Except for in France, where mountain rescue services are provided by the PGHM and are free, all rescues in Switzerland and Italy can be charged for. Even in France, if a doctor has to attend a rescue with PGHM, this may be billed for. In Italy, rescue is generally free if you are hospitalised, but not if due to negligence.

It is therefore essential that anyone planning the TMB should obtain adequate insurance for mountain rescue, the cost of which could well be in excess of £10,000. Insurance should also cover you for any associated medical treatment needed.

TOUR DU MONT BLANC
INFORMATION AND ADVICE

What terrain to expect in the Alps

The TMB is largely on well-formed trails, with only a few short sections of more technical trekking. There are some small fixed ladders to negotiate between Aiguillette d'Argentière and La Tête aux Vents (waypoints 139–140), from Chéserys to Lac Blanc (waypoint 142) and from Col du Brévent to Brèche du Brévent (waypoint 154). There are also some rockier boulderfields to negotiate on Fenêtre d'Arpette (Variation 5) and La Tête aux Vents from the Col des Montets path (Variation 8), and some short rockier steps near Col du Bonhomme (waypoint 30) and Tête de la Tronche (waypoints 76–77). These sections, where significant extra care needs to be taken, amount to just a few hundred metres over the course of the TMB so the TMB is not classified as anywhere near as technical as the Haute Route in France and Switzerland or the GR20 in Corsica, though both these routes are worthy next objectives if you enjoy the TMB.

Around twenty per cent of the TMB is on farm tracks, where you can walk two abreast, and this includes delightful sections such as from Notre-Dame de la Gorge to Refuge de la Balme (waypoints 20–25), or from just below Col de la Seigne to Lago Combal (waypoints 47–50). This makes the TMB a more sociable trek for friends or groups, as you aren't in single file all the time.

Walking poles are used by the vast majority of those on the TMB, and are of great assistance on rougher ground, or when crossing streams or snow patches. The one thing that many people note on the TMB are the lengths of some of the descents, and the impact that has on their knees. The longest descent is from just below Le Brévent at 2,525 metres (waypoint 156) down to the finish at Les Houches at 1,008 metres, but there are also several short and steep descents such as from Plan Checrouit down to Dolonne (waypoints 62–65).

The snow patches that are still present early on in the season create their own objective dangers. There is plenty of scope for a long slip if you're not careful. There are a few steep traverses where extra care needs to be taken when there is still snow such as from Col du Bonhomme towards Refuge du Col de la Croix du Bonhomme (waypoints 30–33), from Col du Brévent to the ladders and piste behind Le Brévent (waypoints 153–156), or the optional descent from Col des Fours (Variation 2). These have sadly all seen fatalities over the years, but with due care and attention can be crossed safely.

Trekking through Arp Vielle Inferiore (waypoint 51). © *Kingsley Jones.*

Greater risks are posed by early-season snow bridges across streams which, if they collapse, could plunge someone into the water under the snow, from which there would be no escape. Some key crossings to be cautious of in early season are Nant des Lotharets (waypoint 31), Ruisseau des Tufs (Variation 2), Ruisseau du Roget (waypoint 44), and the stream below Rifugio Elena (waypoint 88: the bridge mentioned in the route description is installed once the snow has sufficiently melted to allow this; before this has happened there is a tricky stream crossing here). There are of course more in early season, but the key rule is not just to blindly follow other footsteps, but to consider a higher or lower track, well clear of any melt hole that is indicative of a weak snow bridge.

Equipment lists and what to take

For walking or trekking the TMB where you are staying in mountain huts along the trail, you should aim to carry a sensible minimum, which can easily pack into a small twenty-five or thirty-litre rucksack. Don't forget that all bedding is provided in huts (except for a sleeping bag liner), and you can generally arrange to leave extra baggage in your initial accommodation at Chamonix or Les Houches while out on your trek.

When staying in mountain huts, hut slippers (such as sandals or crocs) are generally provided for you to wear indoors, so you don't need to carry any spare footwear. Be aware that if you are staying in hotels in towns such as Courmayeur this will not apply. All drinking water in huts is potable, so water filters or purification tablets are unnecessary. There is no need to carry smarter clothing to wear in the evening at mountain huts – you'll be disappointed if you do, as no one else will have made the effort! Also, most mountain huts have a good stock of cards and games to play in the evenings; you'll become an expert at *Uno*. You'll find travelling light easy if you stay in mountain huts as bedding and food is provided. See pages 10–12 for more details of what to expect when staying in mountain huts.

If you are camping or backpacking then your bag will roughly double in size. See our kit list for the extra items you'll need to carry. For more details on campsites and wild camping see pages 13–15.

Trail runners and fastpackers can adapt our kit list to suit their requirements. A rucksack will typically be replaced by a twelve-litre race vest or up to a twenty-litre running bag. Walking trousers can be replaced by running tights. All items in the clothing and safety sections should be carried, albeit lightweight versions. If going very lightweight you can ditch the travel towel (use your spare base layer), toiletries, travel wash, anything required for snowy conditions, and extra small comfort items, such as a sleeping mask. A good guideline is to always carry the UTMB obligatory kit list items at all times; see ***www.utmbmontblanc.com/en/UTMB*** However, it is worth remembering that on a UTMB race event there is significant temporary infrastructure on the route for the runners, such as refreshment points. Obviously this is not there when you are running or fastpacking the TMB independently, so you need to pack more than the obligatory UTMB kit requirements to ensure your safety.

There's always debate about which footwear is most suitable for the TMB. A safe rule of thumb is to only consider walking boots with good ankle support until early July, when there is likely to still be significant snow on the route. Trail running shoes or trekking shoes can sensibly be used from early July onwards. Walkers and trekkers should only consider trekking shoes rather than walking boots if they are used to travelling in this type of terrain, or there might be too much strain on their ankles. Remember that during the UTMB in the last week of August, thousands of trail runners will be on the paths in their trail shoes, but they have specifically trained in these shoes in mountain terrain. Minimalist shoes for barefoot hiking or running have no place on the TMB for safety reasons. The granite of the trails is too rough, and they offer insufficient traction on snow. Conversely, maximalist footwear is increasingly popular on the TMB trails, as they provide great cushioning.

These recommended kit lists for walking or trekking can be adapted by fastpackers and trail runners, and are endorsed by our equipment partner Alpkit – the ideal resource for sourcing equipment for your adventure. ***www.alpkit.com***

TMB kit list for walking or trekking
Safety
- Map & compass
- Whistle
- Mobile phone & charger (with European plug adaptor, if required)
- Head torch (& spare batteries)
- Trekking poles
- First aid kit & blister kit
- Medication (if required)
- Survival blanket
- Winter equipment (if required – crampons/micro-spikes, gaiters, ice axe)

Essentials
- Toiletries & wet wipes
- Travel towel
- Travel wash
- Sleeping bag liner
- Sleeping mask
- Ear plugs
- Camera
- Sunscreen

Food and drink
- Water bottle
- Snacks

Clothing
- Rucksack
- Waterproof rucksack liner
- Walking boots or trail shoes
- Waterproof jacket
- Waterproof trousers
- Walking trousers and shorts
- Wicking top x2
- Insulating layer
- Socks and underwear x2
- Gloves and warm hat
- Sunglasses
- Sunhat

Paperwork
- Passport and visas
- Bank card
- Cash (euros and Swiss francs, including small notes)
- Proof of activities insurance

Extra gear for camping or backpacking
- Tent/bivouac bag
- Sleeping mat
- Sleeping bag
- Stove
- Cooking gear and utensils
- Food
- Trowel

Training for your trip

It's very easy not to train enough for the TMB. It's a 169-kilometre route with over 10,000 metres of height gain, and equivalent descent. For most people the TMB is a goal that they have planned for many months, and your training should start early on in the planning stage. It takes the body many months to build up its endurance, especially with back-to-back days, and long ascents and descents on the consecutive days to contend with. By slowly building up your endurance and fitness, you will be able to move comfortably within your aerobic threshold, thus

Trekking tips

- *Gaffer tape* – wrap a two-metre length around your trekking poles, just below the handle. It's a great way of always having some to hand to fix a rip in some gaiters, a boot sole that has come loose, a leaky water bottle, or any other items that need fixing while on your TMB. It's useful for first aid too; it can keep a dressing in place.
- *Maximalist footwear* – while lightweight footwear dominates the headlines, maximalist cushioned shoes and boots are perfect for the rocky trails of the TMB, as they cushion the soles of your feet and protect them from bruising from sharp granite rocks that form much of the trail. The cushioning also helps reduce the impact on your knees.
- *Knife* – carry a small pocket knife to eat your lunch in the mountains like a local. Buy cheese from a farm, and some saucisson and a baguette, then cut slices of the cheese and sausage to eat on your bread. It's far more civilised than trying to gnaw your way through a block of cheese.
- *Sunglasses* – while you aren't on snow for any significant amount of time on the TMB, you'll be gazing at the brilliant white mountains and glaciers, and the glare allied with strong UV, can make your eyes sore. Take some sunglasses rated at category 3 or 4 to fully protect your eyes.
- *Paperwork* – you need to carry your passport or ID card and proof of activities insurance with you on the TMB. Keep these documents dry either by wrapping them in plastic film or keeping them in a ziplock sandwich bag. Take a photo of these documents on your phone so you have a backup. You'll need these items if you plan to travel through the Mont Blanc Tunnel, or to get medical attention, and sometimes even to check into a hotel.
- *Currency* – it's possible just to take euros as currency on the TMB, if you don't wish to take out any Swiss francs. All the accommodation providers in Switzerland who don't take bank card payments will accept cash in either euros or Swiss francs. The shops in Swiss villages such as La Fouly and Champex-Lac are all used to accepting euros, though note that any change will be given to you in Swiss francs.

promoting quick recovery and allowing you to enjoy the experience much more. A key element in preparing for your TMB could be to cut out or reduce the use of cars before your trip, to allow time for your legs to build their natural strength.

Hill training is especially useful, to replicate the type of terrain that you will encounter; two or more consecutive long training days in the mountains will reap rewards. Beware of overdoing resistance training, where you elect to carry heavy loads in the hills, as it can damage your joints and back. However, it is very useful to become better accustomed to hiking with a rucksack on. The key to better enjoyment of the TMB is twofold: firstly to prepare your kit carefully so you're not

A selection of TMB signs. © *Kingsley Jones.*

carrying a heavier rucksack than you have to, and secondly to build up your fitness before you start, so you can concentrate on enjoying the amazing scenery you'll see on the TMB.

If starting from a low level of fitness, it is always worth seeking medical advice before you start training for the TMB. The majority of people who fail to complete the TMB drop out through lack of training, rather than any injury. Good long hikes or trail runs in the mountains before your trip are the best preparation. You'll build fitness, but also develop better balance, footwork and ankle strength.

Navigation and waymarkers

Start in Les Houches, with the big white mountain on your left, and keep turning left as you hike, until you recognise where you are again! Trite though this may sound, navigation on the TMB is very easy, and the waymarking and signposts along the route improve year on year. Even in very poor visibility, the trail is obvious, and if you ever walk for longer than twenty minutes without seeing a signpost or waymark, something has gone wrong. Having said that, don't be complacent. A small cosmetic dusting of snow can occur at any time of year, as can thick fog or cloud, hiding the paint markers on rocks, leaving you reliant on other navigation methods. For this reason, always carry a separate full route map and compass, as mountain rescue would deem you improperly equipped without, which could prove a very costly error in countries where avoidable rescues may be charged for.

Granite is the main rock type of the Mont Blanc Massif, where magnetised minerals in the rock can cause magnetic deviation; however, the TMB largely avoids the granite geology, as it skirts around the massif. In regions such as the Aiguilles Rouges, where you encounter granite, the magnetic variation is so small as to be discounted, especially as those trails are so evident and well maintained too.

On the TMB the marking of the trails varies slightly but is straightforward. On some sections where you are following a Grande Randonée (GR®) long-distance trail, such as the TMB sharing the GR5 between Les Houches and the Refuge du Col de la Croix du Bonhomme, the signs and often rocks next to the trail are marked with place names and a red and white line. Many locations on signposts are preceded by the letters TMB. In Italy the most popular markers are yellow background diamond shapes, bordered in black and with TMB stencilled across the middle. Swiss signposts also mention TMB after place names. Another more unified logo is featuring more and more on the TMB signposts, which is a green square, with TMB stencilled across the middle, with a swirling arrow encircling it.

When it's good weather, navigation is generally as simple as looking for the next major objective or hut marked on a map, and the frequent signposts will guide you to it, often with annotations to suggest how long it will take. This guidebook has numbered waypoints as well as numerous timing points for groups of different speeds to calculate realistic timings; see pages viii–xiii for more details.

Mountain skills

For the TMB, the trails are not really technical; however, you should be aware of a few key mountain skills to keep safe, and if unsure you should seek training on them before you start out.

Objective dangers

In the generally anticyclonic weather patterns of the summer months, the key risk of weather is from afternoon convective storms, which can be quite violent with significant rainfall and lightning risk. These storms are fairly predictable, generally happening in the mid- to late-afternoon. You get plenty of warning as the evaporation on a warm day causes convective clouds to bubble up, first on the warmer southern slopes. The clouds darken as they get heavier, and the storm is then imminent. On each day of the TMB, you should aim to be comfortably installed in your accommodation for the next night before these storms begin. Rockfall is a relatively low objective risk on the TMB, but the key areas to watch out for are when people are above you on zigzag trails, such as approaching Col du Brévent (waypoint 152) or when ascending from Rifugio Elena to the Grand Col Ferret (waypoints 89–92).

Snow patches

These are more frequent in early season, and largely consist of old spring snow that is slowly melting back. In a couple of areas they can be notoriously steep and slippery, such as on the La Ville des Glaciers side of Col des Fours (Variation 2) or on the Champex-Lac side of the Fenêtre d'Arpette (Variation 5). Even on these sections, crampons are only exceptionally required on the TMB; micro-spikes generally suffice. Often the most tricky snow patches to negotiate are not these large snowfields, but short or steep sections of harder snow or ice, such as on snow accumulations over streams, or the short traverse from the Col du Bonhomme towards the Refuge du Col de la Croix du Bonhomme (waypoints 30–33). Trekking poles are invaluable aids to crossing snow patches – push the lower pole into the *névé* and brace your downhill foot against it. For those of a more nervous disposition, an ice axe in early season isn't a silly idea, or plan your route to cross snow patches later in the day, when they have softened up slightly.

Stream crossings

The stream crossings which must be made on the TMB are normally no more than ankle depth in normal conditions. However, mountain weather doesn't always behave itself, and streams rise quickly into torrent, especially in late afternoon storms. Use trekking poles to lean on, and never contemplate crossings if the water is above knee height. If in doubt, wait for the water levels to subside, or if it's safe you might try ascending up the watercourse to where it is shallower to make a crossing feasible. On a very few days a season, the streams of the TMB rise into spate and should only be crossed on secure bridges.

Ladders and fixed equipment

In a few sections of the TMB there are ladders bolted into the rock to aid you up steeper pitches, and a few places where chains or cables are attached to the mountainside to provide a handrail across more exposed sections. These are infrequent, and often the cause of far more discussion than they merit. They are all frequently checked, very well maintained, and no section should occupy you for more than thirty seconds. However, if you are very unhappy with exposure, perhaps a more confident member of your team could carry a short rope, or a long sling, to assist you.

Mountaincraft is a difficult concept to describe but, even on a relatively benign route such as the TMB, good footwork, efficient pacing and a constant awareness of the constantly evolving weather and objective risks are essential. These skills come from spending time in the mountains and, although the TMB is busy and not technical, a good basic level of skills will keep you far safer and make your trek much more enjoyable.

Cairn on the TMB path from Le Brévent to Refuge de Bellachat, with Mont Blanc beyond (waypoint 157). © *Kingsley Jones*.

Guided or self-guided?

It is a legal requirement for those guiding the TMB to be properly qualified, insured and medically trained. Those guiding groups will all wear their UIMLA pin or badge with pride. It's taken these guides several years of significant experience, training and assessment to gain their qualification, the highest award for leading trekking groups internationally. In addition to their badge, they'll have the necessary paperwork for taking paying guests in each country, such as the *Carte Professionnelle* in France. There are frequent controls to find unqualified paid leaders, who face imprisonment. Professional guides typically charge €200–300 per day in the Alps.

There's no requirement for anyone to hire a guide to lead them on the TMB, but the advantages are having someone who not only shows you the way, but can tell you about the route, and the rich tapestry of history, landscapes, individuals and cultures. Their local knowledge enables you to enjoy the trail, without any planning or research. To find a guide for the TMB, visit ***www.baiml.org*** or ***www.uimla.org***

The majority of people who undertake the TMB are self-guided; with proper planning and preparation, there's absolutely no reason not to enjoy it this way. It can give you more flexibility, and a group size and dynamic of your choice.

Baggage transfers

A growing trend on the TMB is for people to elect to stay in hotels in the valley each night and organise for their luggage to be transported from hotel to hotel each day by road. This means that you can carry a lighter bag during the day and stay in more spacious accommodation in the valley at night. The downside is that you miss out on staying in unique and wonderfully located mountain huts and have the added hassle of travelling to and from the route at the start and end of the day.

This guidebook has been designed to take you on the best route for the TMB, not necessarily the best for where luggage vans can follow you. However, if you do require luggage transfers, the route description and accompanying map can help you to identify possible options.

Accommodation

Most people doing the TMB stay in mountain huts; however, there are other options available. In this section we consider the facilities for each type of accommodation, as well as explaining what to expect when staying in mountain huts. Accommodation on the TMB is at a premium; ensure that you book early (around six months in advance for popular mountain huts) to avoid disappointment.

Mountain huts

These vary from purpose-built huts such as the Rifugio Bonatti or Refuge de Bellachat, to old farm buildings that have been converted such as Refuge des Mottets or Refuge de Nant Borrant. Typically the capacity of mountain huts varies from around twenty in the smallest, to over a hundred in the largest. While the buildings may be different, the key elements they provide are the same. There's free drinkable water in all mountain huts, as well as toilet facilities, showers, and a hut team who cook and clean.

Most people stay half board (*demi-pension*), which includes a good evening meal, bed and breakfast. Evening meals are typically three or four courses, and if pre-booked the huts can usually cater for vegetarian and vegan diets. There's no expectation for you to dress up in the slightest for dinner; most people wear shorts and their base layer tops. Huts always provide slippers or crocs to wear, so you don't need to carry spare shoes. The tables in the dining rooms are generally shared with other groups, and it's a nice experience to share your tales of the day over your evening meal. Sometimes you meet people who you'll see on other occasions later on your TMB.

Favourite mountain huts

- **Refuge du Col de la Croix du Bonhomme (WP33)** – the highest mountain hut on the TMB; and while basic in some aspects, such as solar-heated showers, the spectacular location and stunning scenery make this a very special place to stay. To wake up high in the mountains, with slopes frequently full of ibex, is a unique experience.
- **Rifugio Elisabetta Soldini (WP48)** – nestled below the Ghiacciaio d'Estellette and the Ghiacciaio della Lex Blanche, this mountain hut is literally situated on the slopes of Mont Blanc. It's famed for its terrace where you can enjoy some home-made cakes and a beer after a long day out on the trail.
- **Rifugio Bonatti (WP82)** – this hut stands out as the jewel in the crown of the TMB. It is a beautifully constructed hut with walls decorated with photos of the legendary mountaineer and explorer, Walter Bonatti. Enjoy outstanding views of the sunrise on Mont Blanc, and across to the south face of Grandes Jorasses.
- **Gîte d'Alpage Les Ecuries de Charamillon (Variation 7)** – this is a former farm on the slopes of the Le Tour ski area; it has very good food for those staying overnight or passing by for a lunch stop. There are great views down the Chamonix valley to Mont Blanc.
- **Auberge la Böerne (Variation 7)** – this old Savoie building, with its wood panelled walls, is quirky yet welcoming, and offers a real feeling of stepping back in time. It sits in the hamlet of Tré le Champ at the head of the Chamonix valley, close to the Col des Montets.
- **Refuge de Bellachat (WP158)** – 'perched' is the best word to describe this mountain hut; it is on the ridgeline above Chamonix, at the start of the final long descent down to Les Houches. The wooden hut is held on to the mountainside by wires, to secure it in storms. There is a great balcony overlooking the Mont Blanc massif – always a great spot for sunset photos.

The showers vary from unlimited hot water, to token operated, and even solar showers, so check before you plan a half-hour wash. Towels and toiletries aren't provided. Evening meals are generally served around 7.00 p.m. – if you think you are going to arrive later than 5.00 p.m. it's worth calling ahead to let them know you are still on your way.

In mountain huts, the beds vary from bunks to single beds, or sleeping platforms. Each person has their own mattress with sheet, duvet and pillow provided. Huts require you to bring a sleeping bag liner for comfort and hygiene. If anything huts are too hot rather than too cold at night, so often you only need to sleep in your sleeping bag liner. Take some ear plugs if you are a light sleeper as, even in the small rooms, you may hear a heavy snorer in a nearby room.

Breakfast is generally light continental, with cereal, bread and jam, as well as a choice of tea, coffee or hot chocolate. Each hut varies when it wants the bill paid, but the most common time is after the evening meal, to allow you to add any drinks (alcoholic or soft) to your tab. The higher huts mainly only accept payment in cash, but the lower ones sometimes offer payment options by card too. The cost for staying half board in huts varies between around €45 and €70 per night; Swiss huts are generally more expensive than French or Italian huts.

To summarise, you don't need to take anything to stay in mountain huts, apart from a sleeping bag liner and a head torch to find the bathroom at night. Everything else is provided. There's generally access to a shared charging point for phones or electronics, though many walkers take a USB power bank as a backup. Where huts are 'off grid' their electricity is from a generator, so electricity may only be available at specific times.

Most mountain huts don't have WiFi, though this is slowly changing. All the high huts on the TMB have phone signal, apart from at the Refuge du Col de la Croix du Bonhomme, where you have to go to the nearby helicopter landing area or the ridgeline above the hut for a good signal.

A top tip is to put on your warm jacket and pop out of the hut after dinner or before breakfast, as it's a magical time for getting great photos of the sunsets and sunrises in the Alps. By staying in the mountain huts on the TMB, you get to watch the ebb and flow of daylight, and to totally immerse yourself in the mountains of the Mont Blanc massif. It's also a great time for spotting wildlife, when there's no one around to disturb it.

Hotels

For those seeking a greater level of luxury or comfort, as well as small rooms, it is possible to plan a TMB trek staying in hotels each night. There are two compromises to consider; firstly that, by default, you are staying in the valley floors each night, and so will miss the most spectacular views from the higher huts, and secondly that, due to the geography of the TMB, you will need to consider a couple of longer stages between hotels, or even a taxi diversion off the route to reach a suitable hotel.

The most affected section is that from Les Contamines-Montjoie to Courmayeur (waypoints 13–68). This is approximately three days at walking speed; the usual solution for this section is to stay in two mountain huts (either the Refuge du Col de la Croix du Bonhomme (waypoint 33) or the Auberge de la Nova or Les Chambres du Soleil in Les Chapieux (waypoint 36) on the first night; then either the Refuge des Mottets (waypoint 41) or Rifugio Elisabetta Soldini (waypoint 48) on the second night). As none of these classify as a hotel, except for Les Chambres du Soleil which only has a few rooms, the most common solution for this section if you require hotel accommodation is as follows. On the first day walk from Les Contamines-Montjoie (waypoint 13) to Les Chapieux (waypoint 36), then get a bus or taxi to Bourg-Saint-Maurice for a hotel. On the second day return to the route

Trail runners on the slopes of Testa Bernarda (waypoint 76). © *Kingsley Jones*.

at Les Chapieux and walk to Lago Combal (waypoint 50); from here walk on to La Visaille and then get a bus or taxi to Courmayeur for the night. On the third day return to the route at Lago Combal then walk to Courmayeur (waypoint 68).

Hotels on the TMB are generally pleasant and clean, but rather functional; if you want a more luxurious standard of hotel you are restricted to a few in Chamonix, Les Contamines-Montjoie, Courmayeur, Champex-Lac and Argentière. In between, you can select some small, generally family-run hotels, which are used to the needs of those completing the TMB. Without too much effort, you can select a level of luxury on a TMB to suit your requirements.

Campsites

There are many commercial campsites around the TMB, as well as some authorised camping areas. For the latter, look out for signs stating *Aire de Bivouac* or *Camping Autorisée*. Many people are choosing to camp while they are doing the TMB, either due to the limited capacity of increasingly busy mountain huts or simply as a cheaper alternative. The authorised camping areas are all equipped with toilets and washing facilities, and the commercial sites have much more extensive facilities including showers, communal kitchens and recreational facilities.

Campsites are mainly in the valley floors, though some such as those near Refuge de Nant Borrant and Refuge de la Balme (waypoints 24–25) are in the upper sections of the valley, so are much cooler in the hot summer months.

Best places to go wild swimming

- *Lacs Jovet* **(WP26)** – in the Réserve Naturelle des Contamines-Montjoie, the two larger lakes here are both popular for wild swimming. The lakes are surrounded on three sides by a horseshoe cirque of mountains: a beautiful location for swimming.
- *Lac de Mya* **(Variation 2)** – this is a small detour off the TMB, situated at 2,393 metres. The lake is beautiful, though quite shallow, so often warm. After a swim you can head down a faint path in an easterly direction to reach Le Chantel then continue to La Ville des Glaciers.
- *Lac de Champex* **(WP114)** – there are pedalos and rowing boats for hire here, but for some the cool, emerald green waters are too much to resist. While it's not strictly wild swimming, as the village is tucked around its edges, this lake sees plenty of swimmers.
- *Lac de Catogne* **(WP131)** – a short detour to the north of the main route, a swim in this beautiful little lake provides welcome relief after a hot ascent up the TMB trails to the Col de Balme. The dam at Lac d'Emosson is visible from its outflow.
- *Lacs des Chéserys* **(WP142)** – above La Tête aux Vents, these lakes are tucked away, and often calm. There are five lakes to choose from, with the highest one right next to the trail at 2,210 metres. This one gets great reflections of Mont Blanc in it.
- *Lac du Brévent* **(WP157)** – a short detour from the main route on the way from Le Brévent to Refuge de Bellachat, this lake has a very remote feeling to it, with views across to the Rochers des Fiz. Due to its northerly aspect, this lake often retains ice in it until July, so it's a chilly dip.

Wild camping

As well as staying at official campsites, it's impossible to ignore the growing demand by those wanting to complete their TMB by wild camping each night. Let's start with the local laws.

France – Wild camping in the mountains is authorised between sunset and sunrise. Be aware that when in nature reserves, such as Aiguilles Rouges or Carlaveyron, camping is not permitted, although bivouac shelters are allowed for the night between 7.00 p.m. and 9.00 a.m. There are a few rangers in these reserves, who can impose fines.

Italy – Technically wild camping is not authorised below 2,500 metres, which would limit you to very few spots on the TMB.

Switzerland – Wild camping is not officially authorised.

Now let's consider the realities. Every night of the season, many tens of people wild camp around the TMB, and they leave no trace, and cause no harm, or are even spotted. Much depends on how sensitively you camp, and how visible you are. Rangers, farmers, police and the authorities generally cast a blind eye to wild campers who are discreetly sited away from the TMB trail, who remove all rubbish, bury all waste and who do not start fires.

There are some amazing places to spend the night, with access to plentiful natural clean running water, and good protection from the wind. A quick look at the map, and you'll start to identify some suitable areas quickly. What historically has caused some issues, and which may further restrict liberties in the future, is careless or lazy wild campers pitching virtually on top of the trail and leaving signs of their stay; stove-burnt grass, broken glass or human waste. Remember to leave anywhere which you wild camp in exactly the condition you found it.

Wild camping the TMB can still be done with a relatively lightweight bag, so plan ahead well, and don't carry too much. There's no sadder sight than some backpacker swamped by the size of their rucksack, struggling up the first climbs of the TMB. Pack right, and you can reduce a rucksack to a more reasonable fifty-litre size for wild camping on the TMB.

Eating and drinking

Food

The variety of local food around France, Italy and Switzerland is one of the most defining and attractive features of the TMB. It has been said by many groups completing the TMB that it was hard to finish weighing in any lighter than when they started. For those who define a good holiday partly by the range and quality of food they eat, the TMB is sure to please. One of the things you will notice is the almost fierce pride which the farmers and locals have in their regional produce. In a world that is saturated with ubiquitous prosaic brands, the food of the TMB shines out. Enjoy it, as it is one of the key elements of the whole experience.

Starting in France, the Haute-Savoie is famed for its mountain dishes of meat and cheese, such as tartiflette or raclette. Speciality cheeses are the creamy Tomme d'Alpage and the rich Beaufort cheese, which you can buy direct from the dairy farm at La Ville des Glaciers. Across the border into Italy, the Val d'Aosta is famed for its dried meats and Fontina cheese. Courmayeur has excellent pizza restaurants and several gelaterias. The streets are filled with the aroma of freshly ground coffee wafting from the café doorways. In Switzerland, the mountain food of the Valais region is notable for fondue and rösti, and the Martigny area and the Rhône valley produce some great wines from vineyards first planted in Roman times.

On the descent to Arnuova Desot (waypoint 84). © *Stephen Ross*.

When you book accommodation on the TMB, all mountain huts and most hotels offer a half-board package, which includes dinner, bed and breakfast; see pages 10–13. For lunches there are three options to consider.

Packed lunch – Mountain huts all advertise that you can order a packed lunch with them when you arrive, to take with you the next day. The typical cost is around €10 or €15. If you plan to order a packed lunch, don't leave it until the morning to request it from the hut, as they are generally prepared in the kitchens while breakfast is served.

Lunch in a mountain hut – All the mountain huts you pass on the trail serve lunches. The advantage of this approach is that you order what you want, rather than a fixed packed lunch provision, and the costs are similar. Not to mention that this choice saves you carrying a packed lunch, which gets progressively sweaty in your pack on a hot day. The disadvantage is that you risk having to wait a while for your food to be served.

Al fresco – If you want to keep costs down, and to eat out on the mountain-side, many opt to purchase a few supplies from shops as they pass by, to make lunches from until the next resupply. There are groceries shops in Les Houches,

Les Contamines-Montjoie, Les Chapieux, Courmayeur, La Fouly, Champex-Lac, Trient and Argentière (slightly off the route). Also, you will pass farms selling local produce, such as cheeses and honey.

On some evenings you may elect to stay in towns such as Courmayeur or Chamonix. Both have a vast range of restaurants to choose from, with local and international cuisine to suit all tastes and budgets. Consider just booking for bed and breakfast if you're staying in a town, to allow you to explore the town a little and enjoy a meal of your choice.

Best places to stop for lunch

- *Refuge de Miage* (**WP10**) – nestled in below the summits of the Dômes de Miage and the Aiguille de Bionnassay, this spot is idyllically situated with crystal clear streams and a lovely mountain hut in the alpage surrounded by peaks high above.
- *Tête Nord des Fours* (**Variation 2**) – eat your lunch in one of the most beautifully misanthropic locations on the TMB, with views back down the Contamines valley and ahead into the Vallée des Glaciers above Les Chapieux.
- *Arête Mont Favre* (**WP54**) – this point provides an imposing view of the magnificent south aspect of the Mont Blanc massif.
- *Tête entre deux Sauts* (**WP80**) – this small peak is a short deviation from the TMB route, and offers an isolated perch overlooking the Rifugio Bonatti far below, and beyond to the south face of the mighty Grandes Jorasses.
- *La Giète* (**WP124**) – this small alpage between the Alpage de Bovine and Col de la Forclaz is a haven of peace and lush vegetation. The conifers provide shade on a sunny day to eat and sleep under.
- *Tête de Bellachat* (**WP157**) – far away from the bustling trails of the Aiguilles Rouges, and honeypots such as Lac Blanc, this peak looks directly on to the north aspect of Mont Blanc; you can marvel at the route taken by the first ascensionists, Balmat and Paccard, back in 1786.

Drink

For those who enjoy an alcoholic drink, the TMB region is not dry by any means. If you're keen to sample local produce, there are some great microbreweries in all three countries, as well as regional wines and spirits too. Look out for the Micro Brasserie de Chamonix and the award-winning Big Mountain Brewing Company in France. Enjoy the Genepì, Limoncello or Grappa of the Val d'Aosta in Italy, and the Valaisanne ales and Rhône valley wines in Switzerland. Most mountain huts have beer on tap, and there's always bottles of ale or wine available to buy. The highest mountain hut on the TMB is the Refuge du Col de la Croix du Bonhomme at 2,443 metres, and even it has Leffe on tap. Beware if you are continuing onwards for the night – it's strong stuff!

Water

Along the TMB you pass mountain huts every few hours, so can always top up with fresh clean running water from any of them. In addition, there are many water fountains and troughs clearly marked as drinkable water along the trail, as well as specific toilets and water points. If you drink from these sources alone, carrying around 1.5 litres per person will suffice.

There are hundreds of clean mountain streams that you can also drink from and which do not require filtering or treatment. Choose wisely, following the four key rules below, and you'll never have tasted water so clean and fresh. As an added bonus, the supplies are so frequent that you never need to carry more than one litre of water, which lightens your pack.

- Look for clean water without sediment or colouration.
- Check that it's a fast-flowing and a well-aerated (tumbling) stream.
- Check that the stream is flowing over gravel or bedrock, not mud.
- Look up the stream to ensure there is no obvious livestock grazing.

Water weighs one kilogram per litre; carrying too much is one of the surest ways to turn your TMB into a slog. There are a few arid regions to be aware of, such as the Aiguilles Rouges above the Chamonix valley (waypoints 137–164), and the section from Bellevue to Refuge de Miage over Col de Tricot (waypoints 7–10). Refilling your water in mountain huts you pass is always free, whether you are staying there or not, so if you're unsure about judging water quality, you can rely on hut supplies. The only proviso is the Refuge du Lac Blanc (waypoint 143) and Refuge de Bellachat (waypoint 158), which often suffer from limited fresh water supplies; bottled water can be purchased.

Flora and fauna

On the TMB you need to keep your eyes open to look at the sky and cliffs above, as well as the ground below your feet. If you're lucky you'll spot golden eagles, bearded vultures, Alpine choughs, marmots, Alpine ibex and chamois. The almost complete removal of top predators from the Alps, allied with more protection laws, has enabled the numbers of all these species to grow in recent years. None of the wild fauna on the TMB that you will encounter poses any risk to you if left at a respectful distance.

The flora on the TMB encapsulates everything about adaptation and ecozones in the mountains. You pass from subalpine spruce and larch forests which can contain species including the martagon lily and slipper orchid, upwards into the alpine shrub zone of myrtle and rhododendron, then into the true alpine zone. This upper area is just below the snowline (nival zone), and species abound including many gentians, campanula thyrsoides and edelweiss. Higher in this zone you can spot saxifrages and ranunculus glacialis.

On the traverse heading towards Arnuova di Mezzo (waypoint 83). © *Stephen Ross*.

If you're interested in identifying the flora on the TMB, there are many phone apps and field guides to choose from, and soon you'll not only know the differences between your avens and campions, or androsace from toadflax, but you'll learn flowers with medicinal and poisonous and even carnivorous qualities. The knowledge is fascinating, and soon you'll learn to use flowers to tell you the altitude by their range. Others such as the carline thistle will even help you with a weather forecast, by closing with humidity and opening with dry air and higher pressure.

The only animal to be especially wary of is the patou (Pyreneean mountain dog), which farmers use to protect flocks of sheep or sometimes goats. Give the herd a wide berth, moving slowly and averting your eyes. Don't let the dog perceive you as a threat, and they will ignore you. Most farmers are very aware of the TMB season, and it is rare to encounter patou on the key trails, though at the extremities of season they are more common as the livestock is slowly moved down the mountains to the valley floor for the winter months.

Transhumance is the movement of farmers and their animals up the alpages as the snows melt from spring into summer, and the descent in the autumn as the snowline creeps downward once again. The alpages are the upper meadows in which the farm animals graze, and they give the Alps their name. The TMB passes through many stunning alpages, and it's hard not to witness the stereotypical image of cows grazing, with their bells ringing out across the alpages. The grazing herds of cows or sheep you encounter will be far more interested in filling their bellies with lush grass than they are in you passing by.

Environmental awareness

The Alps are sadly a vivid case study of rapid global climate change, with glaciers retreating, seracs tumbling and rockfalls on the high peaks, as the permafrost level races upwards. Despite the rate of catastrophic change, the mountains and vistas of the TMB are still staggeringly beautiful, and we all need to plan how to do a TMB with minimal environmental impact, both on the macro and micro scales. Here are some ideas you can consider.

- *Transport* – travel to the Alps by more environmentally sensitive transport, such as by train, rather than flying.
- *Offset* – calculate the carbon footprint of your travel online and pay an offset contribution.
- *Water* – avoid buying bottled water; refill your water bottle at mountain huts and drink from streams where it is safe (see page 18).
- *Local* – buy food from local suppliers, to support local economies and minimise the environmental impact of long-distance distribution.
- *Rubbish* – take any trash you generate with you and recycle what you can in one of the towns you pass through.
- *Luggage* – only take what you need on the TMB and avoid unnecessary baggage transfer vans.
- *Equipment* – purchase kit from a brand with sustainable credentials.
- *Sensitive* – pick no wild flowers, take no rocks, minimise footprints and leave no trace at all.
- *Footpaths* – keep to the path to avoid erosion; do not cut the corners on zigzag paths.
- *Educate* – spread this message to others on the trail, or via blogs and social media posts.

It's too easy to be sad about the rate of glacial and environmental change in the Alps, but the views are still stunning, and you can enjoy time in many landscapes where the impact of humans is hard or impossible to spot. Listen to the sound of silence, revel in the colours of the flowers, feel the spray of the tumbling waterfalls, touch the textured rocks and breathe deeply on that Alpine air. The TMB environment is a sensory overload; while the global ecosystem is at breaking point, these landscapes give you wellbeing in bucketloads, and a focus of why it is so important to protect it for future generations.

The Alps bear the ravages of the tectonic upheavals that formed them, the quaternary glaciations and alluvial history that ground them down, and now the impacts of humans. But, above and beyond all, these stark mountains have a savage beauty and a plethora of landscapes that never fail to inspire and nurture all those who pass through them.

Characters of the *Tour du Mont Blanc*

- ***Mara Rizzo*** – guardian at Rifugio Bonatti. Mara has a true mountain spirit. She doesn't use an online availability calendar for the rifugio, instead taking bookings by email, so she can connect better with her guests. In the kitchen, she cooks delightful food and she enjoys extending a warm, Italian welcome to her guests.
- ***Kilian Jornet*** – athlete who has won the UTMB three times (2008, 2009 and 2011). Kilian was born in a mountain hut in the Pyrenees, but lived in the Chamonix valley for many years, so the UTMB is a home from home for him. He is also the record holder for the fastest ascent of Mont Blanc. ***www.kilianjornet.cat/en***
- ***Lieutenant Jean-François Martin*** – helicopter pilot, PGHM Chamonix. Jean-François hit the headlines in January 2019 for a skate support helicopter landing on a steep snow slope to rescue an injured skier. He's one of forty mountain rescue team members based in Chamonix, who are one of the busiest teams in the world, working 24/7 and 365 days a year. ***www.pghm-chamonix.com***
- ***Alain Desez*** – mountain guide and pole inventor. Alain has guided on the trails of the TMB and the summits of the Mont Blanc massif for decades, as well as paragliding over them. He invented the revolutionary A2-16 poles, as a result of all his mountain experience, and used them on his multiple finishes of the Tor des Géants. Alain lives in Chamonix. ***www.a2-16.com***
- ***Michel and Catherine Poletti*** – founders of the UTMB ultra trail race. This Chamonix couple also set up the International Trail Running Association. Michel is still a competitive trail runner, and Catherine makes every effort to meet as many UTMB finishers as possible, waiting patiently at the finish arch for hour upon hour. ***www.utmbworld.com***
- ***Rob Farwell and Gen Novak*** – TMB experts. The TMB is a large part of the livelihood of this Chamonix-based couple. Rob is a qualified UIMLA trekking guide who leads groups around the TMB several times each year; he has also run in some of the UTMB series events. Gen is a professional sports photographer, covering some of the ultra-trail events in the region, as well as being a runner too. ***www.alpsadventures.com***

Overleaf: Looking back towards Mont Blanc from Variation 4. © *Stephen Ross.*

Overview map

Looking up the Mer de Glace towards the Grandes Jorasses. © *Stephen Ross.*

| Tour du Mont Blanc |
| Variations |
| V1 |
| S/F Start/Finish |
| → Route directic |

Passy

Saint-Gervais-
les-Bains

V1

Les Contamines-
Montjoie

V2

Col de la Croix
du Bonhomme

Les Chapieux

Route profile

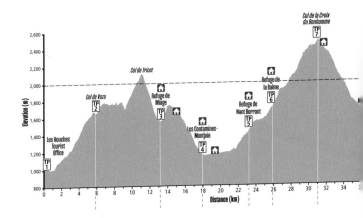

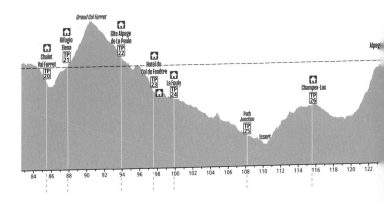

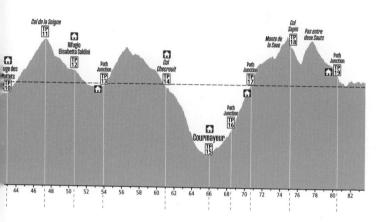

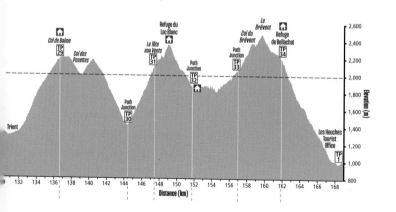

Map legend

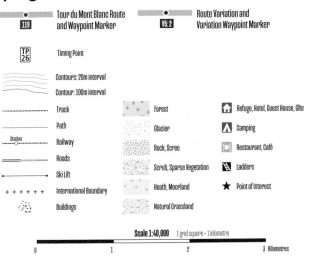

●●●●●● **119**	Tour du Mont Blanc Route and Waypoint Marker
●●●●●● **V5:2**	Route Variation and Variation Waypoint Marker

TP 26 Timing Point

~~~~~~~~ Contours: 20m interval

~~~~~~~~ Contour: 100m interval

Track

Path

Station Railway

Roads

Ski Lift

+ + + + + + International Boundary

Buildings

Forest

Glacier

Rock, Scree

Scrub, Sparse Vegetation

Heath, Moorland

Natural Grassland

Refuge, Hotel, Guest House, Gîte

Camping

Restaurant, Café

Ladders

★ Point of Interest

Scale 1:40,000   1 grid square = 1 kilometre

0   1   2   3 Kilometres

GPS INFORMATION: WGS84/UTM Zone 32N

TOUR DU MONT BLANC
ROUTE MAP AND DESCRIPTION

The TMB is one of very few non-numbered Grandes Randonnées (long-distance trails), which gives you a clue as to its significance. Despite that, there is no 'official' route, and over time some of the trails used to circumnavigate Mont Blanc have fallen out of favour, new ones have been created, and fashions and popularity have altered.

The route described in this guidebook is that which is taken by the majority, along the most scenic trails. For example, most people on the TMB follow the Col de Tricot route from Col de Voza, as it is above the treeline and far more scenic than the Grande Randonnée GR5 route that drops into the Contamines valley. There are a few other route choices within this description that are subjective as to which is the route and what is a variation, but the main route described is the one that is considered to give you the best and most enjoyable TMB experience.

All the mountain huts on the route are listed in the directions, along with a selection of campsites and hotels. For a full accommodation list see pages 108–117.

The waypoint numbers in the route description are shown on the maps in this guidebook. Without further ado, enjoy your TMB.

Waypoints, numbered from **1** to **165**
Timing points, numbered from (TP1) to (TP34)

Towns and villages ◉

Accommodation 🏠

Campsites ⛰

Food and drink 🍴

Points of interest ★

❘ **Shortcut.** //   ❘

Left: Approaching La Flégère with the Mont Blanc massif ahead (Variation 9). © *Kingsley Jones.*

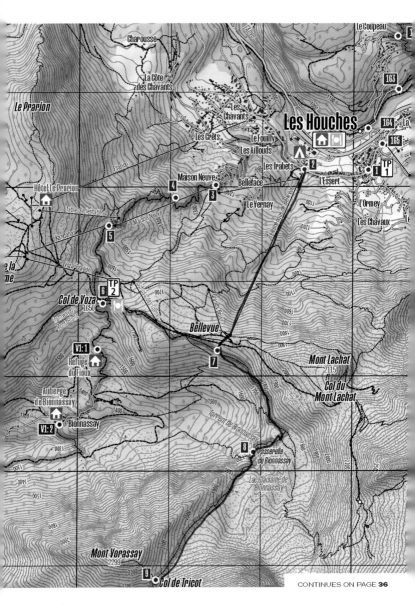

CONTINUES ON PAGE **36**

TOUR DU **MONT BLANC**

Directions

1   (TP1) **Les Houches Tourist Office.** In the centre of Les Houches, next to the tourist office, there is an arch that marks the start and finish of the TMB. With the tourist office on your left, walk along the road. You'll pass a Crédit Agricole cashpoint. Arrive at the Bellevue Cable Car.

> **Les Houches** ⦿ The village is a ribbon development along the main street. The town centre boasts a few shops, supermarket, chemist, bars and restaurants. In the square outside the tourist office is the start and finish arch of the TMB; it's become a selfie-magnet for all those beginning and completing their TMB circuit.

> **Chalet Les Méandres** 🏠

> **Gîte Michel Fagot** 🏠

> **Camping Bellevue** ⛺

2   **Bellevue Cable Car.** Those who wish to avoid the 800m of ascent can take the cable car, but for the purists walk past the cable car station; after around 450m turn left on to a path signposted to *Col de Voza*. The path rises steeply; at Les Crêts turn left along the Route des Aillouds. Continue along the road to reach Maison Neuve.

3   **Maison Neuve.** Go behind the bottom station of the Maison Neuve Chairlift, and veer right on to the gravel 4x4 track. This ascends steeply into the forest and up through the Les Houches ski area. After a sharp right-hand bend the track passes under the Maison Neuve Chairlift, and you reach the old farm buildings at Les Vieilles Luges.

4   **Les Vieilles Luges.** Follow the track steeply upwards as it ascends along the edge of a winter ski piste. Be vigilant on this section as mountain bike tracks cross the TMB here. Keep on the main track and you'll soon reach the bottom station of the Kandahar Chairlift.

> **Hôtel Le Prarion** 🏠 This hotel has wonderful view from its rooms and terrace towards the Mont Blanc massif – it is a short diversion off-route.

5   **Kandahar Chairlift.** Continue on the main track. This area is used for the Alpine Skiing World Cup and, as you pass it, you are on the final climb towards Col de Voza. Fork right at a junction. Soon you leave the ski pistes behind and Col de Voza comes into view ahead. Turn left to arrive at Col de Voza, where there is a toilet and water point. Turn right to cross the tram tracks and follow the 4x4 track right up to a hairpin.

> **La Rioule** 🍴

VARIATION 1 CONTAMINES VALLEY starts

VARIATION 1 CONTAMINES VALLEY

START WP6 (TP2)   **FINISH** WP13 (TP4)

This variation should be considered if you wish to reduce the amount of ascent in this section, or if there is a risk of inclement weather, especially lightning storms, which would be dangerous on the Col de Tricot. This variation traverses more hamlets and farms, so is a pretty alternative that explores the agricultural nature of the Haute-Savoie region.

6 (TP2) **Col de Voza.** Follow the GR5 trail straight ahead, down the main farm track through a few bends, to arrive at Refuge du Fioux.

> **Refuge du Fioux** 🏠 Situated right next to the route, this comfortable chalet is a nice place to stay away from the busy valley floors, especially if you want to arrive in the Alps around midday and set off straight away on the TMB, but just have a few hours on the first afternoon.

V1:1 Refuge du Fioux. Continue straight ahead down the track, passing a large car park on the left-hand side after 600m. Continue straight on, then turn right to arrive in the charming village of Bionnassay.

> **Bionnassay** ⦿ It's hard to believe that Bionnassay was decimated in the glacial meltwater pocket flood on 11 July 1892, when around 200 people died here and lower down the valley in Bionnay and Saint-Gervais-les-Bains.

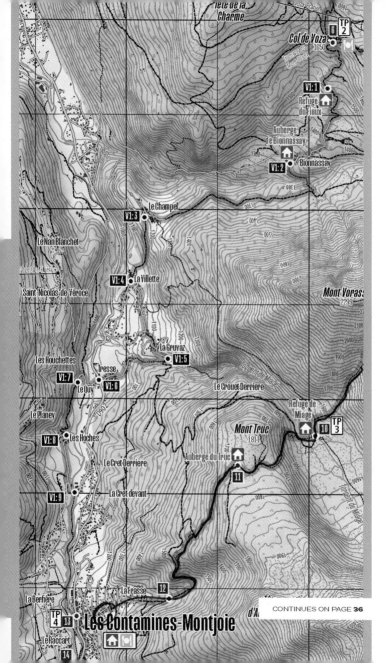

Tête de la Charme

Voza-Prarion

Col de Voza
1650

TP
2

G

Tramway du Mont-Blanc

V1:1

Refuge
du Fioux

Auberge
de Bionnassay

V1:2

Bionnassay

Le Champel

V1:3

Le Nan Blanchet

Mont Voras
2299

V1:4

La Villette

Saint-Nicolas-de-Véroce

La Gruvaz

V1:5

Les Houchettes

Tresse

V1:7

V1:6

Le Quy

Le Crouet Derrière

Le Planey

Refuge de
Miage

TP
3

10

V1:8

Les Hoches

Mont Truc
1811

Le Cret Derrière

Auberge du Truc

11

La Cret devant

V1:9

La Frasse

12

La Berfire

d'A

CONTINUES ON PAGE 36

TP
4

13

Les Contamines-Montjoie

Le Raccart

14

> **Auberge de Bionnassay** 🏠 Originally an eighteenth-century farm, it was converted into accommodation in 1968 as the demand for places to stay for trekkers started to increase.

V1:2 Bionnassay. Turn left off the road on to a path past Chapelle de Bionnassay. Cross the river to ascend on the far side and reach a forest track. Turn right along the track; follow it to Le Champel. Follow the main road through the hamlet until you reach a sharp right-hand hairpin bend.

V1:3 Le Champel. From the sharp right-hand hairpin bend, turn left on a track that descends into the forest then turn left to arrive in the village of La Villette.

V1:4 La Villette. Fork left to head up the road towards La Gruvaz. As you arrive in La Gruvaz turn left then after 200m turn left again. Follow the road right into a large car park at the foot of a gorge.

V1:5 La Gruvaz car park. From the car park, cross the bridge and climb up the track. At the first corner, turn right on to a footpath that becomes a road and drops down to Tresse, where you reach the D902.

V1:6 D902, Tresse. Cross the road and continue straight ahead on to a smaller road, which crosses a stream, curves right and then left, to reach the small village of Le Quy.

V1:7 Le Quy. The road gives way to a farm track, which ascends then traverses the hillside to pass through Les Meuniers, then through a stream valley to arrive at the main road through the village of Les Hoches.

V1:8 Les Hoches. Turn left and follow the road through the pasture. After 500m turn left. Turn left again at the next junction on to Route du Plan du Moulin, pass a timber yard then reach a bridge.

V1:9 Route du Plan du Moulin. Cross the bridge then turn right to follow the riverside track for 1.25km, then turn left following the sign for *Les Contamines*. Turn right along the main road and arrive at the church. This is the end of Variation 1; continue on the main route from Waypoint 13.

1 Suspension bridge (waypoint 8). **2** Metal steps on the trail (waypoint 8). *Both © Stephen Ross.*

6 **(TP2) Col de Voza.** Follow the 4x4 track as it curves round to the left (signposted to *Bellevue*), keeping the tram tracks relatively close on your left-hand side. After 200m take a left fork. After 800m keep straight on then soon afterwards fork left. Follow the 4x4 track right up to a path intersection near the Bellevue Station on the Tramway du Mont Blanc.

7 **Bellevue.** Continue straight ahead. The trail traverses through the woods across a steepening hillside. On some narrow sections there is some fixed equipment and handrails. The path then crosses open slopes to reach the building at l'Are. Go straight on here then after 200m turn right then go straight on to descend steeply to a suspension bridge.

8 **Suspension bridge.** This footbridge crosses high above the tumbling meltwaters of the Glacier de Bionnassay. Cross the bridge; ignore the path on the right leading to Le Champel and continue straight ahead towards Col de Tricot. You soon leave the treeline behind as you climb steadily to the pass.

9 **Col de Tricot.** Continue straight ahead to follow a steep zigzag descent that follows the fall line of the hillside, straight down to reach the chalets and Refuge de Miage at the foot of the slope.

> **Refuge de Miage** 🏠 A stunning place to stop for a snack or lunch, or overnight, with the peaks of the Aiguille de Bionnassay and Dômes de Miage dominant on the skyline.

CONTINUES ON PAGE **39**

10 (TP3) **Refuge de Miage.** There is a water fountain to refill your water bottles here. From the Refuge de Miage turn right before the stream. Cross two bridges then turn left on to the single-track path to ascend the steep slope beyond, signposted to *Chalets du Truc*. Keep on the main path until you reach Auberge du Truc.

> **Auberge du Truc** 🏠 Situated on an alpage plateau, below the small summit of Mont Truc.

11 **Auberge du Truc.** Follow the broad trail out of the alpage and down into the forests. Ignore a forestry access path on the left that inclines upwards. Just after the first right-hand bend, turn left on a small path descending off into the forest; this rejoins the forest track lower down. Keep following the track down until you reach Les Granges de la Frasse.

12 **Les Granges de la Frasse.** Continue straight on to pass the old farm buildings and reach the edge of Les Contamines-Montjoie. Pass the car park in La Frasse (there is a toilet block in the car park), then follow the direct trail that cuts between the road zigzags to reach the main street of Les Contamines-Montjoie next to the church.

VARIATION 1 CONTAMINES VALLEY ends

> **Les Contamines-Montjoie** ◉ Here you will find a supermarket, ATM, shops and a tourist office. It is the last major village until you reach Courmayeur in Italy, so it's an ideal place to stock up with provisions for the next section of the route.

> **Club Alpin Français Chalet des Contamines** 🏠

13 (TP4) **Church of Sainte Trinité, Les Contamines-Montjoie.** Turn left along the main road, passing a ski lift and avalanche/flood barrier, to reach a road bridge.

14 **Road bridge.** Cross the footbridge (just upstream and visible from the road bridge), then turn left on the far side of the river to follow the path to the next road.

15 **Chemin des Echenaz.** Cross the road and continue straight ahead for 200m until the next road.

16   **Chemin des Hameaux de Lay.** Turn left to cross the bridge then immediately turn right on to the footpath. Follow the footpath for 250m until you reach the road.

17   **Route de Notre-Dame de la Gorge.** Follow the road for 250m, until the road bends sharply to the right and you reach Foyer de Ski de Fond.

18   **Foyer de Ski de Fond.** Leave the main road and continue straight ahead along the narrow tarmac road. Follow the forest trails for the next 500m, passing Nordic skiing and biathlon facilities, until you reach Lac du Pontet.

> **Camping le Pontet** ⛰
> **Gîte le Pontet** 🏠 These are situated just off the route in a small leisure complex with tennis courts and play areas.

19   **Lac du Pontet.** Pass Lac du Pontet on the right-hand side; keep on following the path through the woods along the floodplain of the river for 1km, until you see the church of Notre-Dame de la Gorge on the right-hand side.

> **Notre-Dame de la Gorge** ★ Cross the bridge to access the church; there has been a church on this site since at least the thirteenth century. The current baroque church dates from 1699; it has Renaissance frescoes and gilt features.

20   **Notre-Dame de la Gorge.** Continue straight ahead along the steep bare rock of the Roman road. After 1km you will spot a small sign on the right to *Pont Naturel*.

> **Pont Naturel** ★ This rock arch was carved by the river; it is far below you in a deep gorge.

21   **Pont Naturel.** Continue straight ahead on the main path for around 100m; it then curves round to the right to arrive at a stone bridge.

> **Pont Romain** ★ Take a look at the Roman numerals carved into the rock on the bridge. There is also a viewing platform where you get vertiginous views straight down into the deep gorge, with the roaring waters of the river far below. Don't drop your camera!

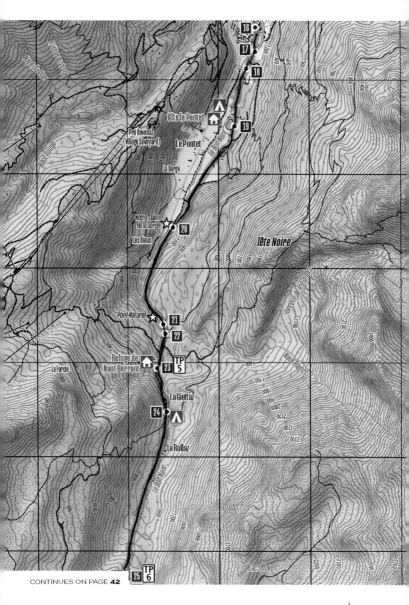

CONTINUES ON PAGE **42**

Setting off from Refuge de la Balme (waypoint 25). © *Stephen Ross*.

22 **Pont Romain.** Cross the bridge; continue straight ahead along the track until you reach the path junction where a path on the right leads to the Refuge de Nant Borrant.

> **Refuge de Nant Borrant** 🏠 This was converted from a farm into a refuge in 1870 and has remained in the Mattel family ever since. This is a beautiful old refuge, with small rooms of between five and nine beds in total.

23 (TP5) **Refuge de Nant Borrant.** Continue straight ahead along the track, which ascends steeply at first, then eases off; as you exit the trees you reach a path junction with the path on the left signed to a permitted campsite.

> **Aire de Bivouac La Rollaz** ⛺

24 **Aire de Bivouac La Rollaz.** This point marks the transition into the upper alpage of La Rollaz; the view opens up ahead to Aiguilles de la Pennaz, with Tête de la Cicle and Col de la Fenêtre on the right-hand side. Continue straight ahead on the main track. At the far end of the alpage, the track steepens to arrive at a bridge, which you cross. Soon after on the left-hand side is a toilet block and water tap; a little further on you reach the Refuge de la Balme.

Refuge de la Balme 🏠 This mountain hut is quite basic, but in a spectacular situation, with the views all the way back down the Contamines valley.

Aire de Bivouac de la Balme ⛺

25 (TP6) **Refuge de la Balme.** At this point the Roman road and farm tracks you've been following give way to single-track trails. Continue straight ahead for 70m then fork left. Initially the trail ascends a ridge past some waterfalls, then on to a series of rocky zigzags upwards to reach an electricity pylon. Watch out for the risk of rockfall from the cliffs on the right-hand side. This is not a section to linger on for long.

26 **Electricity pylon.** As you pass under the pylon, the track soon flattens off as you converge with the stream once again at a small hydroelectric dam. Go straight on at a path junction. Continue straight ahead to enter the plateau of Plan Jovet. You reach a wooden bridge.

Lacs Jovet ⭐ Turn left at the path junction after the small hydroelectric dam in waypoint 26 to reach Lacs Jovet – it's a delightful spot for wild swimming.

27 **Wooden bridge.** This area is a haven for wild flowers. Cross the bridge and continue straight ahead. The path starts to steepen, leaving the marshy ground behind. Fork left then keep on the main path. It becomes increasingly rocky underfoot as you eventually reach a large cairn at the Tumulus Plan des Dames.

28 **Tumulus Plan des Dames.** Local legend has it that this burial mound marks the spot where the remains of two English ladies were found and buried after they perished in a storm in the late 1800s. To ward off evil spirits, it is tradition to add a stone on to the cairn. Continue onwards and upwards; at the far end of the Plan des Dames you reach a stream, Le Bon Nant.

29 **Le Bon Nant.** The water of Le Bon Nant is generally crystal clear, and good to drink. Cross the braided stream. Then continue straight ahead on the path to ascend the far bank, then up a steeper section through a valley; once above this the final slopes towards Col du Bonhomme open out. Here the path is quite eroded, and there are many intertwined paths. Try to avoid further erosion by sticking to the most obvious central trail. Arrive at the Col du Bonhomme.

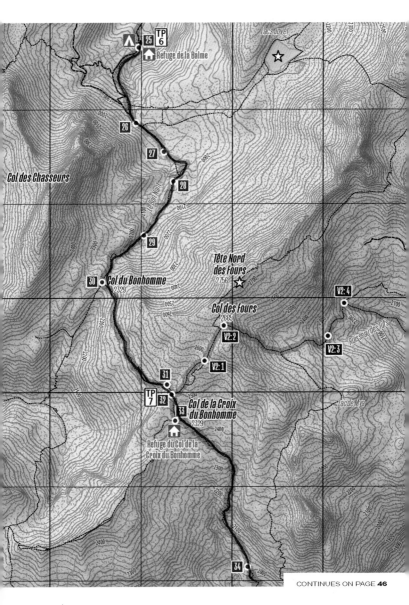

CONTINUES ON PAGE **46**

1 The view from waypoint 30 looking back towards waypoint 29.   **2** Looking south from waypoint 30.   *Both © Stephen Ross.*

30   **Col du Bonhomme.** This pass is the watershed between the Contamines and Chapieux valleys. There is a small shelter on the right-hand side that serves as respite from any rain or wind. From this point, ignore the path that goes straight ahead, and turn sharp left, towards the Col de la Croix du Bonhomme. As you set off from the shelter, just 200m ahead is a rocky step below the Rocher du Bonhomme. This involves a couple of more exposed steps, as the path crosses a steep slope. It can be tricky with compacted *névé* on it; a slip here would have serious consequences. Using a walking pole with your lower foot braced against it offers good security. If the snow is extensive then crampons or micro-spikes may be required. The rock step is soon left behind, and the rocky trail is easy to follow, with dashes of paint on the boulders. Continue straight ahead on the path until you reach a stream.

31   **Nant des Lotharets.** Cross the Nant des Lotharets, which involves a careful hop across from boulder to boulder. Continue straight ahead to arrive at a huge cairn.

VARIATION 2 COL DES FOURS starts

32   (TP7) **Cairn.** Continue straight ahead until you reach the Refuge du Col de la Croix du Bonhomme, more informally known as the Refuge du Bonhomme.

> **Refuge du Col de la Croix du Bonhomme** ⛺ This mountain hut was originally built in 1924; it saw action in World War II with local resistance against the Italian incursion into French territory. The building fell into ruin and was saved initially in 1965 by building works of Franco-German Scouts, then by the Club Alpin Français.

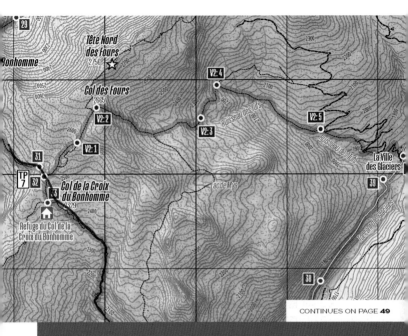

CONTINUES ON PAGE **49**

VARIATION 2 COL DES FOURS

START WP32 (TP7)   FINISH WP40 (TP9)

This high variant of the TMB will appeal to those who want to see one of its most wild and least visited landscapes. The rocky plateau around the Col des Fours is an area of solitude, and the viewpoint of the Tête Nord des Fours is one of the best vistas on the whole TMB. Note that in early season the descent from Col des Fours can be tricky with plenty of snow, and in poor visibility the navigation to the col is sometimes challenging. Opt for this variation on the good weather days, and if you're not put off by traversing often significant snowfields.

32 (TP7) **Cairn.** Turn left towards Col des Fours. Pass under an electricity pylon.

V2:1 Electricity pylon. Continue straight ahead; the path ascends over increasingly rocky ground to reach the Col des Fours. The route is marked with paint marks on the rocks.

Col des Fours (Variation 2). © Stephen Ross.

Tête Nord des Fours ★ At Col des Fours, you might wish to make the optional small out-and-back detour to Tête Nord des Fours, which adds roughly 1km in total to the day, by following the faint path to the left of the col. This summit has a viewing table, and a remarkable panorama in all directions.

V2:2 Col des Fours. Turn right to cross the col; the path dips steeply to the east. Descend towards the Plan des Fours, where the path curves to the left; soon you pass below some waterfalls cascading down the rocky slabs. These are the upper cascades of the Ruisseau des Tufs. Arrive at a crossing point for Ruisseau des Tufs.

V2:3 Ruisseau des Tufs. Cross the stream. Continue straight ahead, with the Ruisseau des Tufs passing through a gorge over to your right, until you reach a path junction.

V2:4 Path junction. Turn sharp right to follow first the right-hand bank, then the left-hand bank of the stream; continue until you reach the farm buildings at Les Tufs.

V2:5 Les Tufs. Turn right then fork right. As the farm track zigzags across the hillside, cut to the right of each corner, and a small path leads directly down to La Ville des Glaciers. Just above the farm buildings of La Ville des Glaciers, you join the farm track for the final bends, and the smell of cheese wafts up to meet you from this famous Beaufort dairy and cheese producing farm below. This is the end of Variation 2; continue on the main route from Waypoint 40.

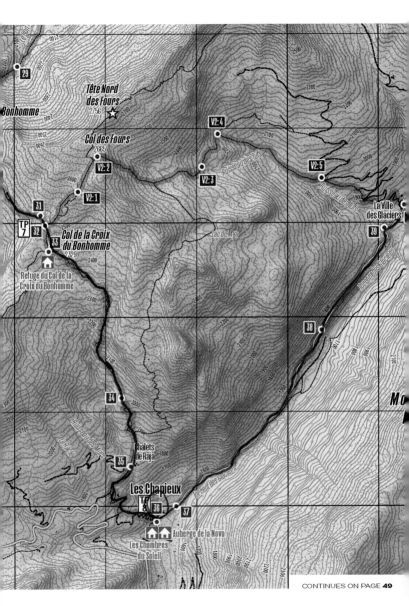

Tête Nord
des Fours
2756 ☆

Col des Fours
2665

Bonhomme

Refuge du Col de la
Croix du Bonhomme

Col de la Croix
du Bonhomme
2329

Lac de Maya

La Ville
des Glaciers

Chalets
de Raja

Les Chapieux

Auberge de la Nova

Les Chambres
du Soleil

CONTINUES ON PAGE **49**

33 **Refuge du Col de la Croix du Bonhomme.** Turn left towards Les Chapieux. The path descends in a south-easterly direction. The trail is interspersed with softer sections and some rocky steps, as you thread your way down near a stream towards the buildings at Chalets de Plan Varraro.

34 **Chalets de Plan Varraro.** Continue straight ahead until you arrive at the Chalets de Raja.

35 **Chalets de Raja.** Just below the buildings you reach a bridge across a stream. Cross the bridge then turn left. Cross another bridge; just before you reach the farm buildings at Les Murs, turn sharp left. The path zigzags down the hillside to reach the village of Les Chapieux.

> **Les Chapieux** ◉ This is the most southerly point of the TMB; there is a small shop, toilet block and water point as well as a field where camping is permitted and other accommodation. If a higher standard of accommodation is required, it is possible to travel by bus or taxi to Bourg-Saint-Maurice.

> **Auberge de la Nova** 🏠

> **Les Chambres du Soleil** 🏠

36 (TP8) **Les Chapieux.** Turn left along the main road through the village. As you leave the village you'll spot a war memorial on the right-hand side.

37 **War memorial.** During World War II the Chapieux valley saw the local resistance stopping the Italian incursion into the Savoie, with several fierce skirmishes. Continue straight ahead up the road (alternatively, there is a trail to the right of the road); after 2.5km you will see a dam wall and hydro reservoir behind it on the right-hand side.

38 **Barrage de Séloge.** Continue straight ahead on the road, passing through Le Chantel. Just after Le Chantel the road bends left then right and you reach a bridge over the Ruisseau des Tufs.

39 **Bridge over Ruisseau des Tufs.** Cross over the bridge and continue along the road; after 300m you arrive at La Ville des Glaciers.

VARIATION 2 COL DES FOURS ends

La Ville des Glaciers ⦿ While evocatively named as the *Town of the Glaciers*, it's neither a town, nor are there glaciers nearby. It is however the dairy farm of the local Beaufort cheese, and you can go into the farm to see how they make the cheese and buy yourself a good slice for lunch on the trail. In one of the farm buildings is a huge copper cauldron where the milk and whey are heated. Across the farmyard is the cheese store, where big rounds of cheese are turned and flipped daily, to prepare them for sale on the market days in Bourg-Saint-Maurice.

40 (TP9) **La Ville des Glaciers.** In the car park there is a toilet block and water point. Turn right and cross the bridge, then turn left to follow the track upstream, following signs for the *Refuge des Mottets*. Continue straight ahead, crossing a number of small streams. After 1.2km you will reach and cross the Ruisseau du Grand Praz, the last stream before Refuge des Mottets.

Shortcut. // If you don't wish to visit the Refuge des Mottets: around 75m after crossing the Ruisseau du Grand Praz turn right, following a TMB sign. Turn right again to rejoin the main route after Refuge des Mottets.

Continue straight ahead for 150m to arrive at Refuge des Mottets.

Refuge des Mottets ⌂ This hut was originally a farm, and some of the large dormitories are the former cowsheds. It's one of the most authentic old huts on the TMB, and the evening meals are always good here. There's also a more modern building for those seeking a greater level of creature comforts, with small rooms and showers.

41 (TP10) **Refuge des Mottets.** Turn right to head up a series of steep zigzags. At the top of the zigzags there is a signpost.

42 **Signpost at the top of zigzags.** Turn left, traversing more gently up the hillside. In places there is duck boarding to protect the soft ground from erosion, so please stick to the trail. Continue as the path veers to the right across steeper ground into a stream valley. In early season this can retain snow patches; and care needs to be taken to select a route with a good snow bridge over the stream beneath. Arrive at a stream.

Col de la Seigne
2516

ITALY

FRANCE

Refuge des Mottets

La Ville
des Glaciers

Col de l'Oullion
2695

CONTINUES ON PAGE **51**

1 Looking back down the zigzags towards Refuge des Mottets (waypoint 42). © *Stephen Ross.*   **2** Aiguille Noire de Peuterey from Arp Vielle Inferiore (waypoint 51). © *Kingsley Jones.*

43 **Stream.** Cross the stream and continue straight ahead. The path climbs steeply at first, then contours around into the rocky valley of the ephemeral stream, the Ruisseau du Roget.

44 **Ruisseau du Roget.** Cross the stream and continue straight ahead. After a steep section the path curves around to the right and the gradient eases, leading up to the Col de la Seigne, which is the Franco–Italian border.

45 (TP11) **Col de la Seigne.** There is a border stone and a large cairn to mark your entry into Italy, but there isn't any formal border infrastructure. Along the border at roughly 100m intervals are the ruins of old fortifications. You won't be paying attention to the border though, as towering above is your first view of the majestic Italian side of Mont Blanc. The scale is vast, with a vertical drop of over 3000m from the summit to the valley floor. Continue straight ahead to descend eastwards into Italy; the trail takes you past a building, La Casermetta.

46 **La Casermetta.** This is a small environmental education centre; in case of a storm it can be used for shelter. Continue down the path, and you will cross a bridge a reach a path junction.

47 **Path junction next to stream.** Visible up to your left are Les Pyramides Calcaires, a limestone intrusion that is a marked difference to the red granite of the Mont Blanc massif behind them. Continue straight ahead, passing some ruined buildings at Tza de la Blanche. In the alpage you will see piles of stones that look like dinosaur eggs. They're nothing of the sort, merely the farmers clearing land to allow grasses and flowers to grow to feed their herds. Continue along the path until you arrive at the ruined buildings at Lex Blanche.

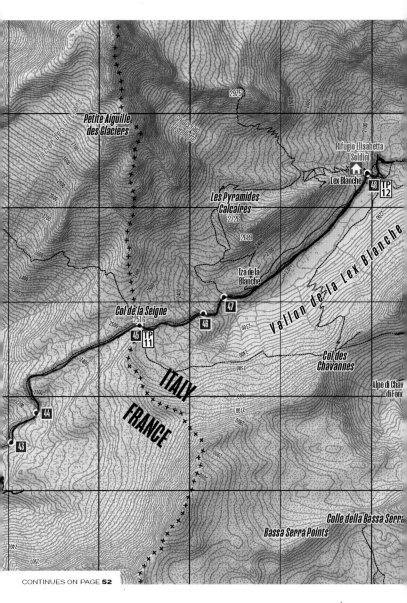

CONTINUES ON PAGE **52**

CONTINUES ON PAGE **55**

1 Rifugio Elisabetta Soldini (waypoint 48). **2** Bridge at waypoint 49. *Both © Stephen Ross.*

> **Rifugio Elisabetta Soldini** 🏠 Situated very close to the route, this spectacularly located mountain hut is accessed up a rubble track. The setting is magnificent, with a stunning backdrop of mountains and the icefalls of the glaciers providing a rumbling soundtrack throughout the day.

48 (TP12) **Lex Blanche.** Ruined buildings are perched on the end of this hanging valley, where once the Lex Blanche glacier would have surged into the valley. Turn right to follow the trail down the zigzags below the mountain hut, and you arrive at a path junction on the impossibly flat valley floor, and the straight line of the Strada Lago Combal track.

49 **Strada Lago Combal.** Continue straight ahead to follow the Strada Lago Combal track for 2km, to reach a path junction at the far end of Lago Combal. This is a glacial lagoon caused by the Ghiacciaio del Miage blocking the valley, and the alluvial outwash of the upper valley glaciers filling in the upper Val Veny. Lago Combal is shallow and offers great photo opportunities with the mountains reflected in the water.

> **Shortcut.** // If you wish to avoid the next mountainous section, go straight ahead here and cross the bridge. Continue to La Visaille, where you can get a bus to Courmayeur.

> **Lago del Miage** ⭐ It's worth a walk up the glacier moraines to see this glacial meltwater lake.

> **Cabane du Combal** 🏠

50 (TP13) **Lago Combal.** Turn right at this signposted junction; continue until you reach the ruins of an old farm at Arp Vielle Inferiore.

1 The needle of the Aiguille Noire de Peuterey (waypoint 51). **2** Lago Combal (waypoint 50). © *Both Stephen Ross.*

51   **Arp Vielle Inferiore.** Continue upwards on the trail; it steepens past a ravine and then curves to the right. You arrive at a stream, which marks your entry into the upper alpage above the treeline.

52   **Stream.** If there are no grazing herds above you, refill your water bottle from the stream, as it is cool and clean. Cross the stream and continue upwards on the trail, with the stream to your right until you arrive at a shepherds' hut at Arp Vielle Superiore.

53   **Arp Vielle Superiore.** This is one of the best sections of the TMB; follow the trail to head upwards, then cutting left, then around to reach the Arête Mont Favre ridge. The views ahead to Mont Blanc are stupendous.

54   **Arête Mont Favre.** After the obligatory photos on the arête, it's time to concentrate again, as the first section of the descent is steep and rocky. Continue along the trail; after just a few zigzags the gradient eases off and you reach a stream.

55   **Stream.** Cross the stream on stepping stones and continue along the path. At the junction fork left (the path to the right goes to Col de la Youlaz). Continue for 350m until you reach Lac des Vesses.

> **Lac des Vesses** ★ This area is a haven for spotting marmots, as they scamper amongst the rocks, beneath which their burrows are safety situated well away from eagles who hunt for them. The first clue you'll get of marmots in the vicinity is a shrill whistling, alerting their family to the presence of danger nearby.

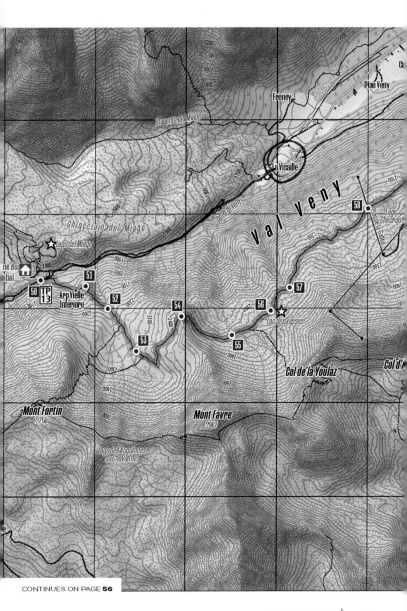

CONTINUES ON PAGE 56

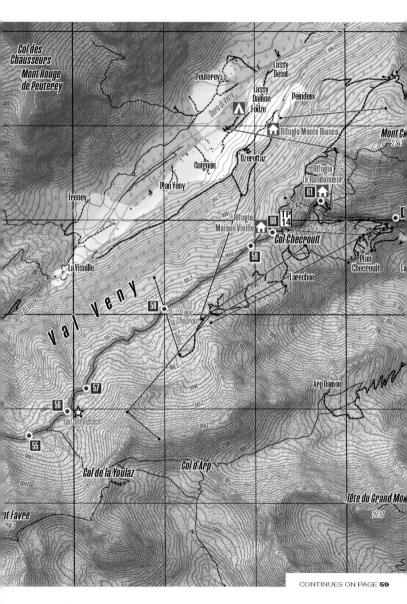

CONTINUES ON PAGE **59**

56   **Lac des Vesses.** Continue for around 350m until you cross a small stream and the Arp Cable Car station is visible high above you to the right.

57   **Path below Arp Cable Car station.** Continue straight ahead to pass under the Plan de la Gabba Chairlift.

58   **Plan de la Gabba Chairlift.** Continue along the trail, passing through the ski area. The views are stunning, especially to the left across to the mighty ridge of the Aiguille Noire de Peuterey. Pass Lago Checrout on the right; the path then dips down below the Bertolini Chairlift and as you exit the trees Rifugio Maison Vieille is visible in front of you. Reach a path junction.

> **Rifugio Monte Bianco** 🏠 To reach this mountain hut, turn left at Waypoint 59 and follow the signs for 1.5km down steep trails.

> **Val Veny campsites** ⛺ There are a few large campsites in the valley; useful as there aren't any on route in this section.

59   **Path junction.** Continue straight ahead to Rifugio Maison Vieille.

> **Rifugio Maison Vieille** 🏠 This is also an aid station on the UTMB; the mountain hut is always festooned with Nepali prayer flags, fluttering in the breeze, with the Mont Blanc massif beyond.

60   (TP14) **Rifugio Maison Vieille.** Follow the 4x4 track straight ahead, passing the top of the Maison Vieille Chairlift, then passing under the Pra Neyron Chairlift. Arrive at Rifugio Le Randonneur.

> **Rifugio Le Randonneur** 🏠 This mountain hut is above the treeline; there are great views across the upper Aosta valley.

61   **Rifugio Le Randonneur.** Continue straight ahead. After 50m turn right at a path junction; this small path drops down, and under the Pra Neyron Chairlift, to arrive at Plan Checrouit, above the Dolonne Cable Car and Courmayeur Cable Car station buildings.

62   **Plan Checrouit.** Continue straight ahead on this single-track trail as it plunges down into the forest. It's steep, dusty and full of tree roots, but soon the steep section is passed, and you arrive at a path junction where our smaller track meets a corner of a 4x4 track.

Rifugio Bertone and Courmayeur far below in the valley floor (waypoint 74). © *Kingsley Jones*.

63   **Path junction.** Turn left on the signposted single-track trail back into the forest. This zigzags its way down, before suddenly emerging at the top of the Dolonne nursery ski area and arriving at a road.

64   **Dolonne nursery ski area.** Turn left along the road; follow it down past the magic carpet ski lift. At the bottom of the ski area you enter Dolonne, which is one of the oldest parts of Courmayeur.

65   **Dolonne.** Continue straight ahead to enter a delightful labyrinth of cobbled streets, with buildings often close enough to touch either side with your arms outstretched. The trail winds its way through alleyways, arches and narrow streets. Navigation is easy, just keep your eyes peeled for the yellow diamond of the TMB which is stencilled on each corner. Almost as suddenly as you enter Dolonne, you exit on to Strada della Vittoria.

66   **Strada Della Vittoria.** Turn left and follow the road as it curves round to the right. Reach a bridge over the Dora Baltea river, which rages through the valley between Dolonne and Courmayeur.

67   **Dora Baltea bridge.** Cross the bridge and continue up the hill on the far side; go through the underpass to reach the Courmayeur Tourist Office.

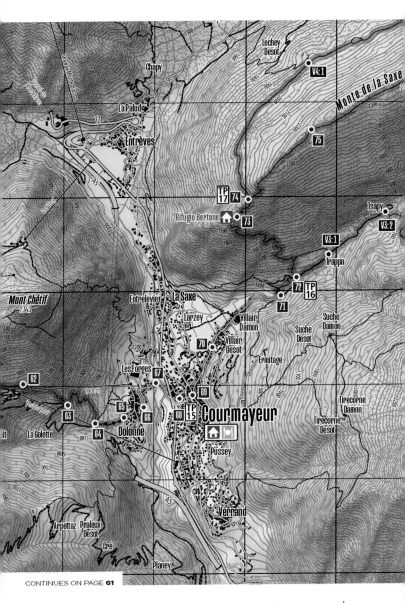

CONTINUES ON PAGE **61**

68 (TP15) **Courmayeur Tourist Office.** Walk past the tourist office along Via Croux; cut through the bus station then continue along the road. Turn left along Via Circonvallazione then turn right into Piazza Brocherel. Continue straight ahead to the church.

> **Courmayeur** ◉ This beautiful town is the largest you'll pass through on the TMB route and has all the shops you could ever need; sports stores, chemists, bakeries, supermarkets, bars, restaurants and gelaterias galore. The main street is cobbled and completely pedestrianised, so you can explore the town with ease.

Grand Hotel Courmayeur Mont Blanc 🏠

Hotel Croux 🏠

Hotel Svizzero 🏠

69 **Church of Saint-Pantaléon, Courmayeur.** Turn left in front of the church on to Strada del Villair, which ascends out of town quickly. Continue straight ahead to arrive at the hamlet of Villair Desot.

70 **Villair Desot.** Continue straight ahead, and there is an almost imperceptible gap between Villair Desot and Villair Damon. Ignore the roads turning off on the right and continue out of the village; 500m later you arrive at the Raffort bridge.

71 **Raffort bridge.** Turn left to cross the bridge and ascend the track. After 150m turn right then continue straight ahead to arrive at a junction marked with a signpost.

VARIATION 3 COL SAPIN starts

VARIATION 3 COL SAPIN

START WP72 (TP16) **FINISH** WP78 (TP18)

On a clear day, the main route is the obvious choice, due to great views across to the Grandes Jorasses from the Monte de la Saxe. If the summits are shrouded in cloud, this variation saves you a fair bit of ascent that is unnecessary if you aren't getting any views. It also stays more sheltered from the wind as it gradually ascends the Val Sapin.

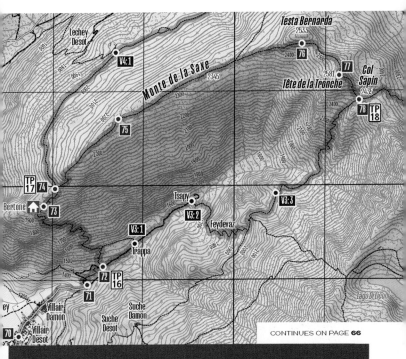

CONTINUES ON PAGE **66**

72 (TP16) **Signpost.** Turn right to head north-east up the valley, keeping the river to your right. The track is good and leads you straight to the cluster of buildings at Trappa.

V3:1 Trappa. Here the track narrows; continue for another 800m to reach a path junction at Tsapy.

V3:2 Tsapy. Turn right to cross the river and up into the forests on the far side. The path steepens and zigzags through the forest until it joins a track. Turn left along the track; continue straight ahead, ignoring a path off to the right, until you reach the farm buildings at Corru.

V3:3 Corru. Continue straight ahead; the path contours around the spur of the hillside. Cross a stream, then the path zigzags to ascend the hillside up towards the Tête de la Tronche, but below the upper slopes the path curves right to contour to Col Sapin. This is the end of Variation 3; continue on the main route from Waypoint 78.

72 (TP16) **Signpost.** Go straight ahead up the hill, and follow the beautiful single-track trail up through the woods. You don't see the Rifugio Bertone until you are fairly close, and you suddenly pop out of the trees into the alpage above. Rifugio Bertone is in a cluster of farm buildings; there are stunning views of Mont Blanc, down the Aosta valley and across to the witch's hat shape of Mont Chétif.

> **Rifugio Bertone** 🏠 Nestled into a small hollow on the ridge above Courmayeur, this mountain hut has spectacular views down the Aosta valley, and towards the Mont Blanc massif.

73 **Rifugio Bertone.** Continue straight ahead on the path to arrive at a path junction with a viewing table and signpost.

VARIATION 4 CONTOUR TRAIL TO RIFUGIO BONATTI starts

VARIATION 4 CONTOUR TRAIL TO RIFUGIO BONATTI

START WP74 (TP17) **FINISH** WP82 (TP19)

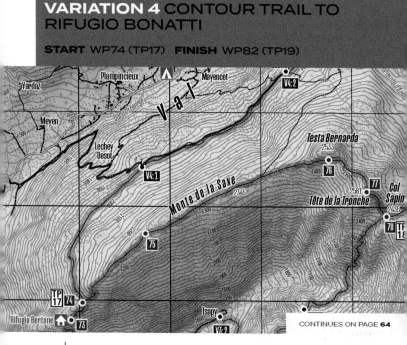

CONTINUES ON PAGE **64**

74 (TP17) **Viewing table and signpost.** Turn right at the signpost; the path ascends very steeply before curving left around the spur of the ridge. The path continues to ascend steeply until 2,200m, where the gradient eases and you emerge on to the broad back of the ridgeline of the Monte de la Saxe.

75 **Ridgeline of Monte de la Saxe.** Follow the broad ridge, and you'll pass a series of wooden avalanche barriers designed to stop dangerous cornices building up. There are also some small lakes on the ridge. Continue over the summit of Monte de la Saxe then contour right to ascend to just underneath the summit of Testa Bernarda.

76 **Testa Bernarda.** Continue straight ahead; the path cuts east across the slopes of Testa Bernarda. In this section you will often see marmots. Continue across the hill, and you reach the ridgeline ahead, where the path veers right up on to a short rocky section to reach the summit of Tête de la Tronche.

Here you have the choice whether to follow the classic TMB trail over Monte de la Saxe, or to take this variation and contour around the hillside to Rifugio Bonatti. The variation is much quicker, but the main route provides far better views as it follows the wide whaleback ridge crest. On a rainy day or if your legs are tired, you might opt for this lower variation. It is the route taken by the famous UTMB, and the quickest way to Rifugio Bonatti. Do note that when it is wet, some of the stream crossings and traverses on this variation become quite muddy, so gaiters or waterproofs may be required.

74 (TP17) **Viewing table and signpost.** Turn left at the signpost to follow a contour trail across steep slopes. It curves to the north and then to the north-east, passing through the Lechey alpage, and onwards to the farm buildings at Lechey Damon.

Camping Grandes Jorasses ⛺

V4:1 Lechey Damon. Continue along the rolling trail as it contours up the wide plateau on the hillside. You cross through a couple of small stream gullies, and after 2km you reach a farm building at Leché.

Camping Tronchey ⛺

V4:2 Leché. Follow the contour trail onwards, taking a left fork just after Leché, following signs for *Arminaz* and *Rifugio Bonatti*. After 800m the trail curves right to enter the Arminaz valley, before descending to the Torrente d'Arminaz.

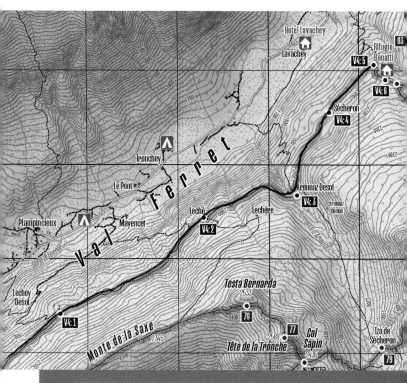

Hotel Lavachey ⌂ This small hotel is a fascinating place to stay, with walls of the bar area covered by historic photos from many generations of the Grivel family, most famous for making ice axes.

V4:3 Torrente d'Arminaz. Cross the stream on a beautiful bridge and take a right fork at the buildings to ascend upwards. Stay on the main path; in 1km you reach the farm buildings at Sécheron. There are often herds of cows grazing in the alpages in this area, but they are generally more interested in their food than they are in you. If shepherds are using their dogs to move herds, keep still and await their instructions as to when it is safe for you to move.

V4:4 Sécheron. Continue along the trail; after 700m you emerge from the woods and arrive at a path junction and signpost, with the Rifugio Bonatti visible above.

Variation 4. © Stephen Ross.

V4:5 Signpost. Turn right then fork right to arrive at Rifugio Bonatti.

> **Rifugio Bonatti** 🏠 A welcome sight at the end of a long day
> – this is one of the best mountain huts on the whole TMB. If you
> are lucky enough to spend a night here, you'll discover why the
> mountain hut is so popular. Even if passing by, it's worth stopping
> for a coffee, or maybe treat yourself with a thick hot chocolate for
> which they are famed.

V4:6 Rifugio Bonatti. Continue on the trail for 130m to arrive at a path
junction. This is the end of Variation 4; continue on the main route from
Waypoint 82.

CONTINUES ON PAGE **69**

1 Mont Chétif viewed from Monte de la Saxe (waypoint 75). **2** Trail runners at Arminaz Desot (Variation 4). *Both © Kingsley Jones.*

77 **Tête de la Tronche.** This is a great spot to take a break, as the views are amazing in all directions. Continue on the path; the descent to Col Sapin is steep and with lots of loose rocks. Arrive at a path junction at Col Sapin.

VARIATION 3 COL SAPIN ends

78 (TP18) **Col Sapin.** Turn left and descend to the east into the Arminaz valley. This is a wild and unspoiled area, and one of the most stunning sections of the TMB. Misanthropes will adore this section; it is quiet because many trekkers follow the lower contour trail (Variation 4) instead. Arrive at the head of the valley floor at the shepherds' hut at Tza de Sécheron.

79 **Tza de Sécheron.** Turn right; the middle section of this ascent is quite steep, but as the path curves right towards the pass the gradient slackens off, and you can take in your surroundings better. Arrive at a path junction at Pas entre deux Sauts.

> **Tête entre deux Sauts** ★ It's worth the short detour off route to take in the view from this small peak.

80 **Pas entre deux Sauts.** Continue straight ahead down into the Malatra valley. In front of you is the massive south face of the Grandes Jorasses. Keep going to reach a path junction just before the farm buildings of Malatra Damon.

81 **Malatra Damon.** Turn left to continue on the trail, passing the buildings of Malatra Damon on your right. Follow the trail over the lip of the upper valley and down the slope to reach a path junction just beyond the ruined buildings at Malatra Desot.

VARIATION 4 CONTOUR TRAIL TO RIFUGIO BONATTI ends

82 (TP19) **Malatra Desot.** If you wish to detour to Rifugio Bonatti turn left and walk for 150m down the hill. Otherwise, turn right on to the track that heads towards the river; cross the bridge and continue to the ruined buildings at Guié Desot.

83 **Guié Desot.** Continue straight ahead up the rising traverse path, ignoring the path dropping down the hillside on the left and crossing several small streams. After 3km you will reach a path junction just before the buildings at Arnuova di Mezzo.

84 **Arnuova di Mezzo.** Turn left and follow the zigzags down the hillside to the tiny hamlet of Arnuova Desot in the valley floor.

> **Chalet Val Ferret** ♠ This small hotel has just seven rooms and is popular with those who are planning bag transfers on the TMB, due to good road access.

85 (TP20) **Arnuova Desot.** This is the location of one of the aid stations on the UTMB. Follow the track for 200m then turn right to cross a bridge. Continue for 250m, you will arrive at a path junction with a signpost.

86 **Signposted path junction.** Turn right up the path; after an initial steep ascent, the gradient eases slightly and you arrive at the building at Tza de Jean Desot. (Be aware that in early season the bridge at Waypoint 88 might not yet be installed, and there is sometimes a tricky snow patch to cross. If in doubt, from Waypoint 86 go straight ahead at the signpost along the 4x4 track to Rifugio Elena. Rejoin the main route at Waypoint 89.)

87 **Tza de Jean Desot.** Continue straight ahead, ignoring the path on the right. Cross a number of small streams then arrive in a small valley with a bridge over the stream.

88 **Bridge.** Cross the bridge and continue to reach Rifugio Elena.

> **Rifugio Elena** ♠ This mountain hut is the last accommodation in Italy – it has great views of the east face of Grandes Jorasses, across to the Ghiacciaio di Pré de Bar and up to Mont Dolent, on whose summit the borders of France, Italy and Switzerland all meet.

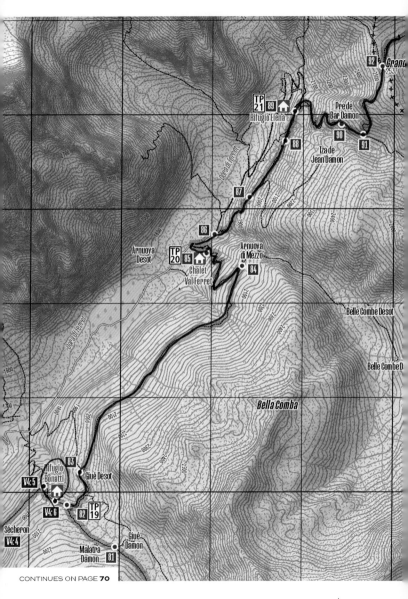

CONTINUES ON PAGE **70**

Les Granges

Gîte de la Léchère

Hotel du Col
de Fenêtre

Ferret

98

99 TP
23

Pas du Dolent

Petit Grapillon
3324

96

97

95

La Dotse
2492

Petit Col
Ferret

Colletto

Tête de Ferret
2744

Arête des Plantins

La Peule

94

Gîte Alpage
de La Peule

93

92

Grand Col Ferret
2537

TP
21 89

SWITZERLAND

Rifugio Elena

88

Pré de
Bar Damon

90

91

Iza de
Jean Damon

ITALY

Col du Bân Darrey

nuova

CONTINUES ON PAGE **73**

1 Approaching Grand Col Ferret (waypoint 91). © *Stephen Ross.* 2 Looking back down the Italian Val Ferret from Grand Col Ferret (waypoint 92). © *Kingsley Jones.*

89 (TP21) **Rifugio Elena.** Continue straight ahead to follow first a wide track and then a single track along the zigzags up the hillside. You ascend upwards above the Torrent de la Combette to reach a small shepherds' hut at Pre de Bar Damon.

90 **Pre de Bar Damon.** Follow the trail across the steep hillside; take care as there is some loose ground underfoot. In 300m you arrive at a path junction.

91 **Path junction.** Turn left. The trail is steep at first as you head up to the edge of a ridge crest, then the path curves right and the gradient eases off as you make the last haul up to reach the Italian–Swiss border at the Grand Col Ferret.

92 **Grand Col Ferret.** Before you drop over the far side, take a look behind you; in the distance you can see the Col de la Seigne, the Franco-Italian border. Ahead of you lies Switzerland. The gradient on the far side is much more benign than on the Italian slopes, and you quickly drop down into the wide rolling terrain. Continue for 1.5km to Creux de la Chaudière, where the gradient steepens.

93 **Creux de la Chaudière.** Follow the trail down into the La Peule valley, on a long descending traverse. Continue for 2km along this path, and you curve gently left around the spur at the end of the valley, and after a couple of zigzags you will arrive at the Gîte Alpage de La Peule.

> **Gîte Alpage de La Peule** 🏠 This hut is a former farm, with the old stables and cowsheds converted very tastefully into dormitories. There are also some Mongolian-style yurts.

94 (TP22) **Gîte Alpage de La Peule.** Take the shepherds' track heading north from next to the yurts belonging to the Gîte Alpage de La Peule. The track traverses the hillside and gently descends; continue for 650m until you reach the narrow valley of the Ravines de la Peule.

95 **Ravines de la Peule.** Cross the narrow valley and follow the narrow trail around the mountainside, over a couple of ephemeral streams, until the trail veers to the right to reach the crest of a spur, the Crêtet de Létemeyre.

96 **Crêtet de Létemeyre.** The trail curves to the left and heads down to the shepherds' hut at Pramplo and a signpost.

97 **Pramplo.** Continue straight ahead on the track down the hillside and into the valley of the Torrent de Merdenson until you reach a path junction at Létemeyre.

98 **Létemeyre.** Turn right and descend to a path junction by a bridge. (Cross the bridge to detour to Ferret village.)

> **Shortcut. //** Ferret is the terminus of the bus that serves the Swiss Val Ferret. The bus runs down the valley to Orsières, where you can change buses to ascend to Champex-Lac, if you wish to shorten the route.

Hotel du Col de Fenêtre 🏠 This traditional Swiss mountain inn has a mixture of dormitory and smaller rooms. It has great views upwards to Mont Dolent.

Gîte de la Léchère 🏠 This is a gem of a mountain hut in a quiet location outside of the villages of Ferret and La Fouly.

99 (TP23) **Bridge.** Turn left and follow the track with the river on your right. After 400m cross a small bridge. Pass the track on your left signposted to Gîte de la Léchère; shortly afterwards turn left on to a 4x4 track. Continue straight ahead through the hamlet of Dessous, and after crossing two tributary streams, arrive at a signpost at Larteron.

100 **Signpost at Larteron.** Turn right and cut down the hillside through a couple of corners; turn left along the riverside track and arrive at the bridge at Le Clou.

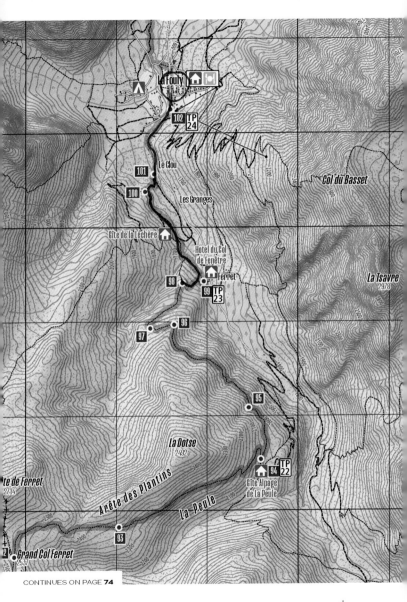

La Fouly

Le Clou

Les Granges

Col du Basset

Gîte de la Léchère

Hôtel du Col de Fenêtre

Ferret

La Tsavre
2978

La Dotse
2482

te de Ferret
2714

Arête des Plantins

La Peule

Gîte Alpage de La Peule

Grand Col Ferret
2537

CONTINUES ON PAGE **74**

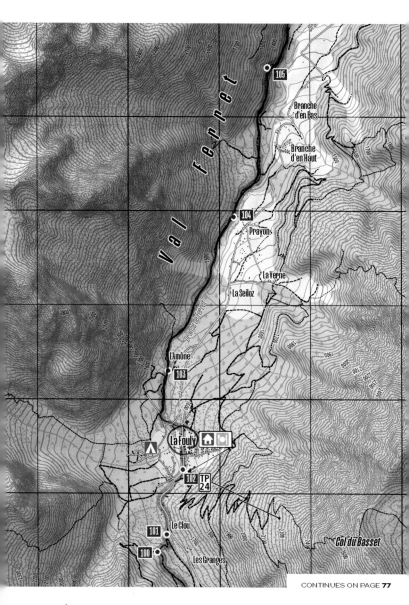

CONTINUES ON PAGE **77**

101 **Le Clou bridge.** Cross the bridge then turn left along the road. Continue along the road to enter the village of La Fouly and arrive at the tourist office on the right-hand side.

> **La Fouly** ⦿ At the foot of the ski lift is an ATM with a toilet block next to it; further along the road is a shop and accommodation. La Fouly is the biggest village until you get to Champex-Lac; this is the place to stop if you need any supplies.

Auberge des Glaciers 🏠

L'Edelweiss 🏠

Chalet Le Dolent 🏠

Maya-Joie 🏠

Camping des Glaciers ⛺

102 (TP24) **La Fouly Tourist Office.** Continue straight ahead on the road through La Fouly. At the far end of the village just before a car park, follow the signposted path on your left. Follow the path down to the river and cross the river on a small barrage. Turn right along the track. After 130m, turn right on to a smaller track that runs parallel to the Dranse de Ferret. Follow the track for 500m until you reach a path junction with a bridge on your right.

103 **Path junction near L'Amône.** Continue straight ahead, keeping the Dranse de Ferret on your right. The path veers to the left away from the main river. Cross a footbridge over the Reuse de l'Amône; the track then curves to the right and continues straight down the valley, running near the river. Follow this track for 1.7km, passing opposite the village of Prayon on the far bank, until you reach a path junction with a bridge on your right.

104 **Path junction near Prayon.** Continue straight ahead, keeping the Dranse de Ferret on your right. After 600m you pass another bridge across the Dranse de Ferret. Continue along the track; as you pass the village of Branche d'en Bas on the far bank the trail enters a rocky ravine in the midst of the forest.

105 **Ravine.** Continue on the trail through the ravine. The trail has some fixed equipment on the left to hold on to if you need it, but the path is stable so this section is passed quickly and easily. On the far side of the ravine you zigzag down a few corners, then continue along the trail for 1.2km until you reach a path junction.

1 On a rocky traverse with chain handrails (waypoint 105).   2 Traditional chalet in Praz-de-Fort (waypoint 107).
Both © Stephen Ross.

106 Path junction. Turn right to follow the path along an amazingly straight
lateral moraine called the Crête de Saleinaz until you reach a path junction
next to a bridge.

107 Path junction next to bridge. Turn left along the riverside path; in 500m
you reach a bridge over the Reuse de Saleinaz. Cross the bridge, and you
enter the village of Praz-de-Fort. Keep right at the principle road junctions,
following the TMB signs, and go into the main old village centre. The
buildings are all traditional farms and chalets, and there are some wonderful
architectural features. When you reach the main road, turn right, then cross
the Dranse de Ferret and almost immediately arrive at a signposted junction
with a tarmac track.

> **Le Portalet cafe/restaurant** 🍽️

108 (TP25) Praz-de-Fort road–track junction. Turn left on to the track
heading north towards Les Arlaches and Issert. After 600m you enter the
beautiful village of Les Arlaches.

> **Croquenature** 🏠 Very small hotel serving home-made
> breakfast and evening meals using fresh, local produce.

109 Les Arlaches. Here the trail traverses the village, and there's a whole host
of traditional features such as old farm buildings, stone water troughs, and
amazing chalet conversions to admire. Continue straight ahead through the
village and carry on along the track. Descend into the village of Issert and
cross a bridge to reach the main road.

> **Café-Restaurant du Châtelet** 🍽️

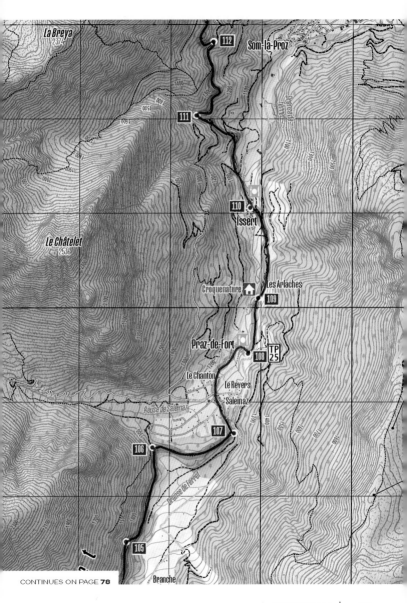

La Breya
2374

Som-la-Proz

112

111

110

Issert

Le Châtelet
2536

Croquenature

Les Arlaches

109

Praz-de-Fort

108

TP
25

Le Chanton

Le Revers

Saleinaz

107

Reuse de Saleinaz

106

Reuse de Ferret

105

CONTINUES ON PAGE 78

Branche

CONTINUES ON PAGES **82–83**

1 Farm building near waypoint 110. **2** Lac de Champex (waypoint 114). *Both © Stephen Ross.*

110 **Issert.** Turn right along the main road and continue for 260m. Turn left on to a side road. Follow it to the first bend and continue straight ahead on to a path and cross the stream. Soon after, turn right on to a path. This traverses upwards and around the hillside to reach a 4x4 track. Follow the track upwards for 300m; at the next junction go straight ahead on a small track into a stream valley to arrive at a footbridge.

111 **Footbridge.** Cross the bridge and head upwards. At the next path junction, fork left and follow it up and through a sharp left-hand bend to another junction. Turn right following the TMB signs to Champex-Lac. After 200m a path joins from the left; continue straight ahead and ignore the path cutting down to the right. Continue until you reach a rock tower on your right at L'Affe.

112 **L'Affe.** Continue along the path, keeping left at the next junction and following the TMB signs up through the final zigzags, above Le Niolet, and quite suddenly you emerge from the forest at the road into Champex-Lac.

113 **Champex-Lac.** Turn left along the road, which turns through a double bend. On the second corner look for a building on the right; turn right on to the path that runs behind the building. Follow the path as it zigzags up the hillside to arrive at a road and buildings at Signal. Turn left and follow the road for 250m to arrive at the edge of the emerald green lake; cross the road on to the lakeside path.

114 **Lac de Champex.** Turn right along the lakeside path. Follow the path to the end of the lake then rejoin the road to continue straight ahead to Champex-Lac Tourist Office.

Champex-Lac ◉ In the centre of Champex-Lac village there are a variety of accommodation options, as well as a bakery and shops. It's the biggest Swiss village you'll pass through on the TMB and is the best place to purchase supplies for the next few days. The village is nestled around a pretty lake; if you've the time spare there's a nice trail around the whole lake.

Pension en Plein Air 🏠

Hotel Alpina 🏠

Hotel du Glacier 🏠

Hotel Splendide 🏠

Camping Les Rocailles ⛰️

115 Champex-Lac Tourist Office. Continue straight ahead along the road; it curves left then right to reach the La Breya Chairlift station.

VARIATION 5 FENÊTRE D'ARPETTE starts

VARIATION 5 FENÊTRE D'ARPETTE

START WP116 (TP26)   **FINISH** WP126 (TP28)

This variation is one of the most challenging sections on the TMB. Only consider it in good weather, otherwise it doesn't merit the extra effort. On good days the views of the glaciers from the Fenêtre d'Arpette are stupendous, and you feel like the ice is close enough to touch. Underfoot this variation has some challenging terrain, both boulderfields and some loose scree, so only consider it if you are adept on this ground.

116 (TP26) La Breya Chairlift station.
Turn left along a path that runs to the left of the station building; almost immediately turn right on to a track that is signposted to the *Relais d'Arpette*. Follow the track for 1.2km then turn right along a road to arrive at Relais d'Arpette.

Relais d'Arpette 🏠 ⛰️ In a lovely situation in the tranquil Arpette valley; small rooms, dormitories and a campsite are available. It has been run by the same family since 1926.

V5:1 **Relais d'Arpette.** Continue straight ahead up the Arpette valley with the stream on your right. Cross the stream at Arpette then continue along the path with the stream on your left at first. Continue for 1.7km until you reach a path junction.

V5:2 **Path junction.** Turn right then shortly afterwards cross the stream. Continue with the stream on your left. Pass the rocky spur of La Barme on your right and arrive at a path junction with the Col des Ecandies path.

V5:3 **Path junction.** Turn sharp right up a zigzag, and then on to a steep and increasingly rocky ascent. Take care in early season when snow patches linger long on these east-facing slopes. Also be wary of this route when there is storm risk, as the jagged peaks of Le Génépi, Pointe des Ecandies and Someceon du Dru are all frequently hit by lightning. Ascend the final steep slopes, and you arrive at the Fenêtre d'Arpette. In front of you, the view of the Glacier du Trient is breathtaking, not that you'll need any more breath taking after the steep ascent.

V5:4 **Fenêtre d'Arpette.** Continue straight ahead to start the descent. The path keeps to the right at the foot of the cliffs, with many small zigzags, then through two main corners, before arriving at the ruined buildings at Vésevey. Here the path leaves the rock and scree behind, and becomes easier, as it descends away from the glacier snout. Follow the trail for 1.9km and you will arrive at the Buvette du Glacier du Trient.

Buvette du Glacier du Trient |●|

V5:5 **Buvette du Glacier du Trient.** You have two choices here. To join Variation 6 turn left towards the footbridge and follow the directions from Variation 6 Waypoint 1. Or to finish Variation 5 and rejoin the main route continue straight ahead along the bisse trail for 2.5km, which is a very gently descending traverse across the hillside, to arrive at a path junction. The bisse is the small water channel alongside the path; it was used to float blocks of ice that had been cut from the glacier down to the Col de la Forclaz, where they were taken on a horse cart to local hotels and restaurants to help store food. This is the end of Variation 5; continue on the main route from Waypoint 126.

MAP IS OVERLEAF, ON PAGES **82–83**

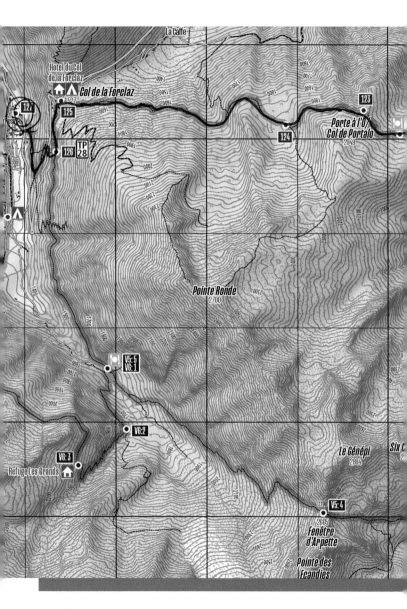

La Caffe

Hotel du Col
de la Forclaz

Col de la Forclaz

127

125

123

126 **TP 28**

124

Porte à l'O/
Col de Portalo
2049

Pointe Ronde
2700

V5:5
V6:1

V6:2

V6:3

Refuge Les Grands

Le Génépi
2884

Six C
2

V5:4

2665

Fenêtre
d'Arpette

Pointe des
Ecandies

CONTINUES ON PAGE **86**

116 (TP26) **La Breya Chairlift station.** Continue straight ahead along the road for 400m; ignore the first forest track on the left then shortly afterwards arrive at a junction with another forest track on the left.

117 **Road–track junction.** Turn left along this wide forest track. Continue for 400m until you reach a path junction with a signpost pointing to the right to *Gîte Bon Abri*.

> **Gîte Bon Abri** 🏠 Set in a quiet hamlet, this gîte offers accommodation in dormitories, small rooms or even a tent in the gardens.

118 **Path junction.** Continue straight ahead along the forest track for 650m then turn right along a track. Cross the Durnand d'Arpette then shortly afterwards turn left on to a narrow road to traverse the village of Champex d'en bas. Continue until you reach a signposted junction with a bridge on your left.

119 **Road–track junction.** Turn left and cross the bridge. At the next track junction keep right then continue for 900m until you reach a track junction at Plan d'en Haut.

> **L'alpage de Plan de l'Au** 🍴

120 **Plan d'en Haut.** Turn left and shortly afterwards pass the buvette and farm buildings at Plan de l'Au. Continue along the track, which goes around the ridge spur and then turns to the south-west. There have been a few landslips on this section over the years; the path becomes single track. The path passes a few stream and winter avalanche gullies before it steepens then curves to the right to cross a larger stream in the Barmay valley. After 250m fork left, staying on the main path, and you arrive at a stream.

121 **Stream.** Cross the stream, hopping across the stones. The path steepens on the far side to climb up away from the stream. You ascend up a series of zigzags through the trees; as you emerge above the treeline you veer to the right across a final stream, and enter the Bovine alpage, where the path gradient eases significantly. At the spur at La Poya the trail curves to the left, then you arrive at the buvette at Alpage de Bovine.

> **Alpage de Bovine** 🍴 Here you can stop off for a bite to eat, and to enjoy some of the best cakes on the TMB.

122 (TP27) **Alpage de Bovine.** Fill up your water bottles here, as the next section passes through a farmed alpage, where there are always livestock

On the ascent to Alpage de Bovine (waypoint 121). © *Stephen Ross.*

above you, and the water quality in the alpage streams can't be guaranteed. The views from here down to Martigny and the Rhône valley are amazing, and you can see the high peaks of the Bernese Oberland. Continue straight ahead. The path contours gently up and through the wide bowl of the alpage to reach the gate at the far end at Porte à l'Ô.

123 **Porte à l'Ô.** Go through the gate, which is designed to keep the cattle in the Bovine alpage, and start your descent through the forest. After 1km you will see the farm buildings of La Giète on your left.

124 **La Giète farm buildings.** Continue straight ahead to pass through this beautiful alpage and on in to the forest at the far side. The path curves around the spur of Les Reblots, which is the most northerly point on the TMB. The path is covered in tree roots in places and you pass several gullies that drop off to the right, but it is a nice descent towards the Col de la Forclaz. After 2km you will notice the trees thinning, and you will see the road converging from the right. Arrive at the road at Col de la Forclaz.

> **Hotel du Col de la Forclaz** 🏠
> **Camping de la Forclaz** ⛺ There has been an inn on this site since around 1830; small rooms, dormitories and a campsite are available.

CONTINUES ON PAGE **90**

VARIATION 6 COL DE BALME VIA LES GRANDS

START WP126 (TP28)   **FINISH** WP131 (TP29)

This variation explores a wilder terrain and is the path less trod. You are rewarded by stunning views of the glaciers and more time above the treeline. To benefit from this time up high, you ascend steeply and quickly soon after the Buvette du Glacier du Trient, so only consider this variation if you've plenty of energy left in your legs.

126 (TP28) Signposted path junction.
Go straight ahead along the bisse trail which goes almost due south for 2.5km. Just before you reach the Buvette du Glacier du Trient arrive at a path junction.

> **Buvette du Glacier du Trient** |●|

V6:1 Path junction. Turn right then cross a footbridge across the meltwater stream from the snout of the Glacier du Trient. On the far side of the bridge turn left towards Les Grands. The track ascends steeply through some zigzags, heading south-east. Arrive at a path junction.

V6:2 Path junction. Turn right to climb upwards towards a cliff line, in seemingly never-ending zigzags. At the final corner, the path curves to the right and ascends a fine stone ramp up the cliff, to arrive at a little cluster of old farm buildings at Les Grands.

> **Refuge Les Grands** 🏠 This is a basic mountain hut, which does generally not have a live-in guardian, but can be booked by telephone. It's a glorious position, overlooking the Glacier du Trient icefall.

V6:3 Les Grands. Despite all the efforts of ascending to here, the wild scenery and solitude more than recompense your ascent. Continue straight ahead to follow the gently descending contour path around the rocky spur of Tronc du Berger, and across the hillside. There are a few small rocky steps to negotiate, but there's nothing too tricky. After passing the ruins at La Remointse, you reach a path junction where you turn left towards Col de Balme. Continue for 2km to arrive at a path junction at Col de Balme. You have two choices here. To join Variation 7 turn left and follow the directions from the start of Variation 7 (beginning at 'fork right on to a path signposted to *Charamillon* and *Le Tour*'). Or to finish Variation 6 and rejoin the main route turn right, passing the Refuge du Col de Balme on your left, and arrive at a path junction. This is the end of Variation 6; continue on the main route from Waypoint 131.

125 Col de la Forclaz. Turn left along the road, walk past a gift shop on the left, then turn left along the signposted TMB trail. Follow this for 550m, and you will arrive at a signposted path junction.

VARIATION 5 FENÊTRE D'ARPETTE ends

VARIATION 6 COL DE BALME VIA LES GRANDS starts

126 (TP28) **Signposted path junction.** Turn right; the path descends steeply through a series of zigzags to reach a footbridge across the road. Cross the footbridge and continue straight ahead on the path into the forest. The path bends to the left; arrive at a junction and turn right on a wide path towards Trient. You emerge on to the road. Turn right and walk for 100m then turn left. Walk for 50m then fork right to arrive opposite the pink church.

> **Auberge du Mont-Blanc** 🏠

> **Hotel La Grande Ourse** 🏠

127 Église Rose, Trient. Continue straight ahead; after 70m the road curves to the left to follow the river. Walk for 450m until you reach a road junction next to a bridge. Turn right to cross the bridge and follow the road for 650m through the village of Le Peuty until you reach a road junction at Refuge Le Peuty.

> **Refuge Le Peuty** 🏠 A very friendly place to stay – it has a yurt in the garden that serves as a dining room.

> **Le Peuty** ⛺

128 Refuge Le Peuty. Fork right on to the TMB track that is signposted to *Col de Balme*, heading south. Cross a small stream then cross the Nant Noir at a footbridge. Turn right after the footbridge to ascend a long series of zigzags through the forest, all the way to the treeline at Chieuset. The path curves south-west to arrive at a path junction at Tsanton des Arolles.

129 Tsanton des Arolles. Continue straight ahead up the easier gradients of the trail. The path converges slowly with the upper valley of the Nant Noir to arrive at the farm buildings at Les Herbagères.

130 Les Herbagères. Continue straight ahead along the track as it zigzags up the hillside. The track then heads south up a spur before it veers west to reach a path junction just north of the Col de Balme.

VARIATION 7 MONTROC DIRECT TRAIL TO TRÉ LE CHAMP

START WP131 (TP29) **FINISH** WP137 (TP30)

This direct route down to the valley is quickest for the poor weather days, or if you are tired. It also passes next to chairlift and cable car stations, so you can opt for a descent in either or both of these. There is a ticket office at the mid-station if you take the lifts down. On stormy days the Posettes ridge is prone to lightning, so this is really the bad weather alternative.

131 (TP29) **Path junction north of Col de Balme.** Turn left to head south passing the Refuge du Col de Balme on your right. Shortly afterwards fork right on to a path signposted to *Charamillon* and *Le Tour* cutting down and away from the main track. Follow this trail for 2km, seeing the buildings of the Gîte d'Alpage Les Ecuries de Charamillon to your left, before you reach a path junction at the cable car and chairlift stations at Charamillon.

> **Gîte d'Alpage Les Ecuries de Charamillon** 🏠 This is a wonderful place to stay or just to stop for lunch – the food is amazing. The gîte has been converted from old farm buildings and has fantastic views down the Chamonix valley to Mont Blanc.

V7:1 Charamillon. Continue straight ahead down the stony 4x4 track. On the second corner after the cable car station turn left on to a path. The path passes under the cable car several times to arrive at a road at Le Tour at the base of the cable car.

V7:2 Le Tour. Continue straight ahead to walk through the cable car station car park and along the edge of the road for 1km to reach a road junction next to the train station in Montroc.

> **Chalets Pierre Semard** ⛺

> **Gîte Le Moulin** 🏠 This gîte is converted from an old water mill building; the evening meals are excellent.

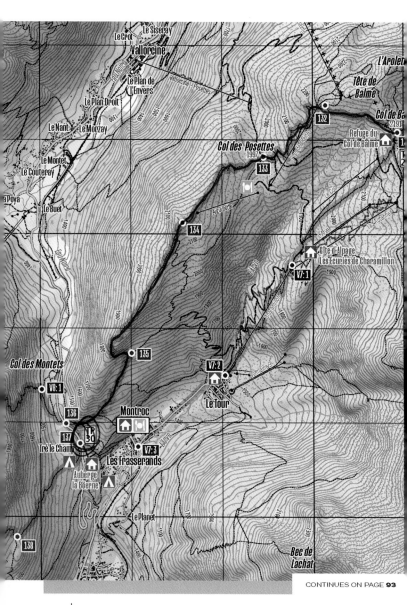

CONTINUES ON PAGE **93**

> **Auberge la Böerne** 🏠 This eighteenth-century wooden farm
> building has been converted into a quirky and pretty place to
> stay. The rooms are accessed by wooden steps, and the auberge
> always serves good food.

V7:3 Montroc. Turn right along Via des Cutes then pick up the trail that curves to
the left to ascend over the roof of the train tunnel, then following a gentle incline to
reach the hamlet of Tré le Champ. Follow the path through the buildings until you
reach a junction with a wide track. Turn right along the track to head north-west to
ascend to a junction with a minor road. Turn right along the minor road to arrive at
the D1506. This is the end of Variation 7. You have two choices: either continue on
the main route from Waypoint 137 or, to join Variation 8, turn right along the road
and walk for 250m until you reach a car park which is the start of Variation 8.

> **Refuge du Col de Balme** 🏠 This mountain hut has recently
> changed hands, and has had a much-needed makeover, after
> years suspended in a time warp.

131 (TP29) **Path junction near Col de Balme.** The Col de Balme marks the
border with France, and ahead of you the view down the Chamonix valley,
and to Mont Blanc ahead, is stupendous. It's the first view of Mont Blanc
since you last saw it from the upper Italian Val Ferret. Turn right and follow
the single-track trail signposted to the Col des Posettes. It traverses the
hillside below the Tête de Balme, and contours across to pass a small stream,
which is the source of the Arve river that flows through Chamonix. Continue
until you reach another stream crossing just before the ski lift lines.

132 **Stream crossing.** Cross the stream then fork left to head down past the
avalanche control fencing, through a series of long zigzags, to reach a jeep
track. Turn right and follow it for 150m to reach the Col des Posettes.

> **Alpage de Balme** 🍴

133 **Col des Posettes.** Turn left to follow the signposted path to the Aiguillette
des Posettes. The path ascends in a series of zigzags to reach the ridge, and
then there is a braided path up the ridge crest. You cross a few rocky steps
and ascend above the top of the Aiguillette Ski Lift to reach the summit of
Aiguillette des Posettes.

134 **Aiguillette des Posettes.** Here there is a magnificent view towards Mont Blanc, across to the peaks towering above the Glacier du Tour and Glacier d'Argentière, and it's one of the best views on the whole of the TMB. After taking in the panorama, continue straight ahead along the ridge. There is an initial rocky section, then you pass a huge boulder to the right, before the ridge crest widens. Follow the ridge down its length to the right of the Tête du Chenavier, where wood steps get you around a steeper section. The path curves to the left around the knoll on the spur, until it cuts eastwards and nearly back on itself. You reach a path junction.

135 **Path junction.** Turn right to head downhill into the trees. Keep right at each of the next two junctions to follow the TMB trail down through the forests to reach the D1506 at a car park.

VARIATION 8 LA TÊTE AUX VENTS VIA COL DES MONTETS starts

VARIATION 8 LA TÊTE AUX VENTS VIA COL DES MONTETS

START WP136 (TP30)   **FINISH** WP141 (TP31)

This variation is for those who wish to avoid the short sections of ladders on the main route.

136 **TP30** **Car park on D1506.** This point marks your entry into the Aiguilles Rouges Nature Reserve. Please note that dogs, even those on leads, are not permitted in this nature reserve. Walk to the far end of the car park and cross the road to go straight ahead along Sentier Botanique. Turn left at the next junction then arrive at a path junction above the Col des Montets.

V8:1 **Path junction.** Turn left and head up the zigzags which ascend steeply up the hillside. The trail is part of the Tour du Pays du Mont Blanc. The path ascends up to the foot of a cliff, and veers left then right to cut around it. Once above the cliffs, the path heads south again on increasingly easier gradients over La Remuaz then Les Deviets.

V8:2 **Les Deviets.** Here there is a rocky boulderfield to traverse. Shortly afterwards continue straight ahead at a path junction. Arrive at the cairn and signpost at La Tête aux Vents. This is the end of Variation 8; continue on the main route from Waypoint 141.

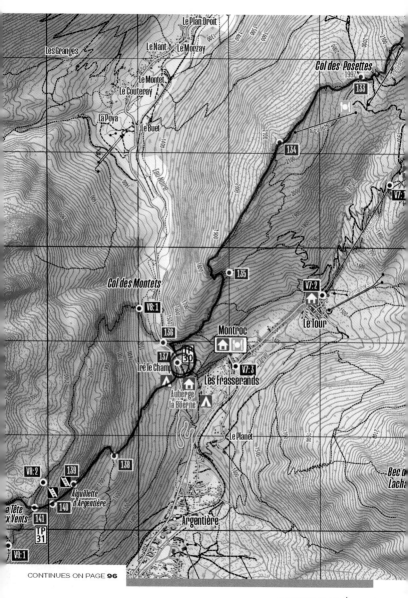

Le Plan Droit
Les Granges
Le Nant
Le Monzay
Col des Posettes
1997
133
Le Montet
Le Couteray
La Poya
Le Buet
134
Eau Noire
135
V7:1
Col des Montets
V7:2
V8:1
Le Tour
136
Montroc
137
TP 30
Tré le Champ
V7:3
Les Frasserands
Auberge
la Böerne
Le Planet
Bec o
Lacha
V8:2
139
138
Aiguillette
d'Argentière
a Tête
x Vents
140
141
TP 31
Argentière
V9:1

CONTINUES ON PAGE **96**

1 Ladders at Aiguillette d'Argentière (waypoint 139). 2 Looking down to Argentière (waypoint 140). *Both © Stephen Ross.*

136 Car park on D1506. Turn left to follow the path at the side of the road for 150m until you reach a small chapel. Cross over the road and continue in the same direction through a car park. At the far end of the car park reach a signposted footpath.

VARIATION 7 MONTROC DIRECT TRAIL TO TRÉ LE CHAMP ends

137 (TP30) Signposted footpath. Turn right on to the footpath heading up into the woods. You soon emerge into a clearing with a stream running through it. Continue upwards, and follow the TMB path for 1km, with a few zigzags towards the end. Arrive at a signposted path junction.

138 Signposted path junction. This point marks your entry into the Aiguilles Rouges Nature Reserve. Please note that dogs, even those on leads, are not permitted in this nature reserve. Turn right to follow the trail up some zigzags towards the foot of the Les Deviets sector of the Chéserys cliffs. The path then curves to the left on a traverse along the base of the cliff line. Ahead of you, a rock needle becomes obvious. This is the Aiguillette d'Argentière.

139 Aiguillette d'Argentière. Follow the path past the needle, and you have arrived at the start of a steeper section through the Chéserys cliffs. The sections of ladders are small, and very securely equipped. There are also some sections of fixed equipment with steel steps, and handrails. Care needs to be taken with this next section of the trail up to La Tête aux Vents, but never is the exposure great, or any climbing skills required. On the ladders, keep three points of contact at all times, and grip the rungs, rather than the edges, to protect you better in the event of a small slip. After you've negotiated the first sets of ladders, there is a small narrow traverse to reach a second set of ladders.

140 **Second set of ladders.** These ascend, traverse, then ascend again. The ladders give way to a series of wooden steps, and you reach a large boulder, which you pass on your right, and arrive at the cairn marking La Tête aux Vents.

VARIATION 8 LA TÊTE AUX VENTS VIA COL DES MONTETS ends

VARIATION 9 DIRECT TO MONTAGNE DE LA FLÉGÈRE ALONG GRAND BALCON SUD starts

141 (TP31) **La Tête aux Vents.** This is a great meeting of paths; the cairn is a popular place for a breather and to take in the view. Continue straight ahead on the trail, signposted towards *Lac Blanc*. After 250m you are joined by another path coming in from the right. Continue to ascend a ridgeline, getting views of the Lacs des Chéserys to your right; after 400m arrive at a path junction.

142 **Path junction.** Continue straight ahead upwards via a rocky section, and as you round a corner, you cross the ridge crest, and a beautiful lake lies below you. Turn left just before the lake to cut around the left edge of the lake; the path then curves to the right and ascends to some more ladders. Traverse the ladders and the wooden steps above, and you will see the buildings of the Refuge du Lac Blanc above you to your left. Continue along the path up zigzags and steps, and you round the final rock slabs to arrive at the refuge.

> **Refuge du Lac Blanc** 🏠 This is a great place to stay with wonderful views over the mountains.

> **Lac Blanc** ★ This is one of the must-see highlights of the TMB – walk around the cobalt blue waters to see the mountains reflected beyond. It's rare to get this place to yourself, but it's justifiably popular; the views across to the north faces of Les Drus and Grandes Jorasses are inspirational.

143 **Refuge du Lac Blanc.** Continue straight ahead to cross the outflow stream from the lake; after 80m you arrive at a path junction. Turn left, signposted towards *La Flégère*. After 300m arrive at a path junction.

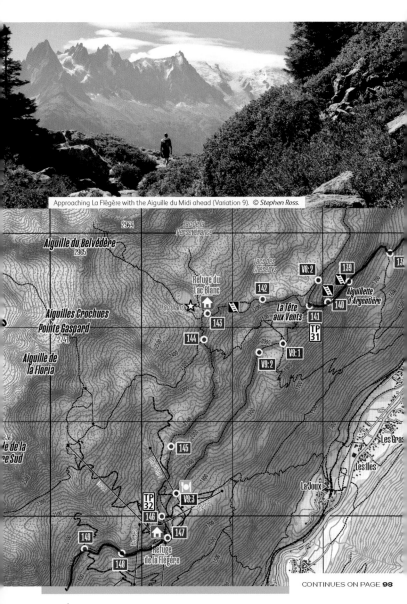

Approaching La Flégère with the Aiguille du Midi ahead (Variation 9). © *Stephen Ross.*

CONTINUES ON PAGE **98**

VARIATION 9 DIRECT TO MONTAGNE DE LA FLÉGÈRE ALONG GRAND BALCON SUD

START WP141 (TP31)   **FINISH** WP146 (TP32)

If you want to cut a corner, this variation takes the direct trail to La Flégère. For trail running fans, this section follows part of the legendary UTMB.

141 (TP31) **La Tête aux Vents.** Turn left and follow the rocky trail to the south-west. There are a few easy rocky steps to negotiate, and you pass some avalanche walls. As you reach a plateau, the trail becomes easier, and you arrive at the building of Chalet des Chéserys.

V9:1 **Chalet des Chéserys.** Continue straight ahead to arrive at a footbridge below a long waterfall that tumbles down a cleft in the cliff.

V9:2 **Footbridge.** Cross the footbridge, which traverses the meltwater stream from Lac Blanc far above you. Follow the trail along the aptly named Grand Balcon Sud, across the Montagne de la Flégère. This is one of the most photogenic trails in the Alps, with the rhododendron flowers framing the dazzling white mountains behind, and the red granite spires of the Chamonix Aiguilles. Continue along the trail for 1.8km, until you pass under the Chavanne Chairlift and arrive at the buvette at La Chavanne.

| La Chavanne |●| |

V9:3 **La Chavanne.** Continue straight ahead to cross the buvette terrace. The path curves around to the left to arrive at a path junction near a small reservoir. Turn right; after 100m arrive at a path junction. This is the end of Variation 9; continue on the main route from Waypoint 146.

144 **Path junction.** Continue straight ahead, ignoring the trail to the right. Soon afterwards, ignore a path turning off on the left. Shortly afterwards you pass a shallow lake on your right. After 800m you pass a cairn marking the edge of the Aiguilles Rouges Nature Reserve. The path veers to the right through the bowl of the hillside to arrive at the Lac de la Flégère.

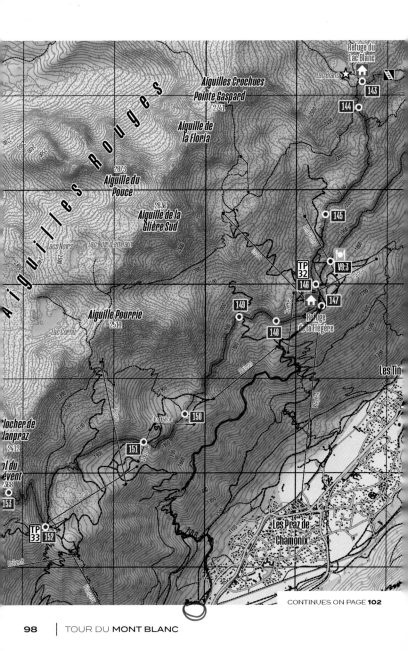

Refuge du
Lac Blanc

Lac Blanc

143

144

Aiguilles Crochues
Pointe Gaspard
2741

Aiguille de
la Floria

Aiguilles Rouges

2873
Aiguille du
Pouce

2836
Aiguille de la
Glière Sud

Lacs Noirs   Lac Noir d'en Haut

145

V9:3

TP
32

146   147

Aiguille Pourrie
2511

149

Lac Cornu

148   Refuge
de la Flégère

Les Tin

150

Chéranon

151   Pierre

locher de
lanpraz
2412

ol du
évent
368

153

TP
33   152

Brévent

Les Praz de
Chamonix

CONTINUES ON PAGE **102**

145 Lac de la Flégère. Continue straight ahead; the path becomes a 4x4 track in the ski area. Pass under the Chavanne Chairlift; shortly afterwards the track bends sharply to the left; fork right on this corner. Continue for 250m to reach a path junction.

VARIATION 9 DIRECT TO MONTAGNE DE LA FLÉGÈRE ALONG GRAND BALCON SUD ends

146 (TP32) Path junction at La Flégère. Turn right on to the 4x4 track; pass under the Trappe Chairlift then go straight ahead towards the Flégère Cable Car station building. Go past the building then turn left, and just below you arrive at the Refuge de la Flégère.

> **Refuge de la Flégère** 🏠 Significant renovations to the mountain hut were undertaken during summer 2019; the adjacent cable car was also completely replaced.

147 Refuge de la Flégère. From the refuge terrace, follow the small single-track trail off to the right, which traverses below the cable car station. You reach a 4x4 track, and make a descending traverse across it, to regain the single track once more. The route is well signposted; follow signs for *Planpraz*. Pass beneath the Evettes Chairlift then shortly afterwards arrive at the top of some steps leading down a steep section.

148 Steps. Descend the steps, and the zigzag at their foot, to follow the path into the Combe Lachenal. There is a boulderfield to cross, which can very occasionally be risky due to rockfall from above, so move continuously across this section. It is quickly crossed; the path then curves around to the left and you arrive at an avalanche wall.

149 Avalanche wall. Cut through the small gap in the wall then continue straight ahead to follow the single-track trail across the boulderfield below the Combe de la Glière. The trail cuts across a series of gullies and spurs to arrive at a wooded treeline, which marks the start of the Montagne de Charlanon. The path descends through some zigzags, and across a jeep track, to traverse a wide bowl winding through boulders. You arrive at a signposted path junction just before the Charlanon Chairlift.

1 Looking across to Mont Blanc with the Brévent Cable Car in the foreground (waypoint 152). **2** Col du Brévent (waypoint 153). *Both © Stephen Ross.*

150 **Signposted path junction.** Continue straight ahead and pass underneath the Charlanon Chairlift. As you round a corner, you suddenly reach a narrow rocky passage, with a fence to your left, around a spur. It's easy to walk through, but the trail is quite rough, so watch your footing. On the end of the rocky section the path traverses up through the forest, with plenty of tree roots to negotiate. As you round a final corner and pass underneath the Sources Chairlift, the dusty trail meets a 4x4 track at a signpost.

151 **Path–track junction.** Turn left along the jeep track then immediately turn right on to a path. Follow this rising path, which is rocky, and curves around the wide gully of the Montagne de la Parsa. You ascend gently to the far side of the bowl, where the path then zigzags upwards to reach a small col, before curving south-west and then south to reach a path junction at the top station of the Parsa Ski Lift. Fork right here and continue for 40m to a signposted path junction.

> **Shortcut. //** To descend directly to Chamonix via the Planpraz Cable Car turn left here and walk for 250m to get to the cable car station.

152 (TP33) **Signposted path junction.** Turn right, signposted to the *Col du Brévent*. After a few initial zigzags you make a rising traverse across the hillside. Watch out for rockfall caused by groups above in this section, especially higher up. After 450m you reach a sharp left-hand bend. Be careful not to overshoot it, as a small path heads off the apex of the corner to some rock climbs. Once round the sharp left-hand bend you are heading south, and then up a series of rocky corners. You reach a ridgeline, with great views ahead, and veer to the right up the final section to reach the Col du Brévent.

153 **Col du Brévent.** The pass is marked by a large cairn; here you meet the GR5 trail coming from the north. Turn left at the cairn and follow the trail. Often there are lingering snow patches in this section, even into August, so take care. Follow the dots of yellow paint on the rocks; you pass through a rocky valley in a moonscape of granite towers. As you ascend out of this valley on the far side, you emerge on to the north-facing slopes below Le Clocher du Brévent. The path is indistinct in places, so keep a good look out for the markers. On the far end of the rocky section, you traverse a steeper slope then a rocky section to arrive at some ladders, the final ones on the TMB.

154 **Ladders.** Ascend the two sections of ladders, taking care as a fall could be serious. At the top of the ladders, traverse to the right and then zigzag upwards to reach a signpost and cairn at the edge of the Brèche du Brévent.

155 **Brèche du Brévent.** Turn right and head up the broad ski piste. As you ascend, you'll spot the railings of the Brévent Cable Car station above you. Arrive at a signposted path junction.

> **Brévent Cable Car station** ★ Turn left at Waypoint 156 to ascend to the top station of the cable car (get the Brévent Cable Car then the Planpraz Cable Car directly to Chamonix if needed) for great views across to Mont Blanc. Le Brévent became popular in the eighteenth century; pioneers ascended the mountain to get a viewpoint across to Mont Blanc in order to help find a route to the summit. The first ascent of Mont Blanc was made on 8 August 1786.

> **Le Panoramic du Brévent** 🍴

156 **Signposted path junction near Brévent Cable Car station.** Continue straight ahead. The path zigzags down granite slabs and across barren slopes. Take care as there are plenty of places to trip on the slabs, but the route is easy to follow. As the gradient eases you traverse below the ridge crest and arrive at a signposted path junction.

> **Lac du Brévent** ★ Turn right at Waypoint 157 to reach Lac du Brévent – this glacial lake offers a splendid panorama of the Mont Blanc massif.

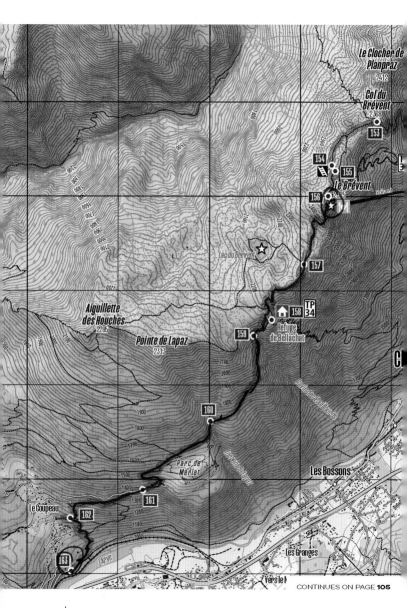

Le Clocher de
Planpraz
2412

Col du
Brévent
2368
153

154
155

Le Brévent
156 2075

Lac du Brévent

157

Aiguillette
des Houches
2285

TP
34
158

Refuge
de Bellachat

Pointe de Lapaz
2313
159

160

Parc de
Merlet

Les Bossons

161

Le Coupeau
162

163

Les Granges

Vers le

CONTINUES ON PAGE 105

157 Signposted path junction. Continue straight ahead; the path rounds a steep corner protected by a handrail, and then doubles back on itself to head towards the Tête de Bellachat. The path curves to the left then zigzags down the slope. You'll gain a glimpse of the roof of the mountain hut below you, before traversing another series of zigzags through an area of braided trails to arrive next to the Refuge de Bellachat.

> **Refuge de Bellachat 🏠** This mountain hut is located in an incredible position, perched on a ridge crest overlooking the Chamonix valley.

158 (TP34) Refuge de Bellachat. This marks the start of the final long descent of the TMB. From the Refuge de Bellachat follow the TMB signs to the west then south towards the valley. Arrive at the Ravin des Vouillourds.

159 Ravin des Vouillourds. Cross the stream. This is rarely more than a trickle of water; its source is a reedy lake, so don't drink the water here, as it's slightly stagnant. On the far side of the stream there is a long set of zigzags that descends the rocky hillside. Eventually you reach the treeline, and the path traverses down through the forests. There are no path junctions; keep going until you arrive at a large stream gully.

160 Torrent de Lapaz. Continue straight ahead. There are some handrails to help you on a rocky zigzag into the gorge; cross the stream then in 150m arrive at a signposted path junction. Fork right at the signpost. The trail skirts around the north edge of Parc de Merlet, a wildlife park; several trails join the path from the right. Keep following signs for *Les Houches* and *Statue du Christ Roi*. Soon the path emerges on to the road leading to Parc de Merlet.

161 Parc de Merlet. Turn right then walk along the road for 180m. Turn left along a signposted path. Keep straight ahead at the next path junction. At the next junction turn left, following signs towards *Statue du Christ Roi*. The trail descends some steep zigzags to arrive at Statue du Christ Roi.

162 Statue du Christ Roi. There's no missing this 25m-high concrete statue, which was built in 1933. Continue along the trail, following signs for *Les Houches*, and you will arrive at some buildings at the foot of the hill in the hamlet of Les Eaux Rousses.

163 Les Eaux Rousses. Continue straight ahead along the main river track until you reach a junction with a road. Turn left and walk along the road until you reach Gare SNCF – Les Houches.

164 **Gare SNCF – Les Houches.** Turn left to cross the bridge over the river then over the N205. At the far side of the bridge follow the road as it curves to the right then to the left to reach the main road through Les Houches.

165 **Rue de l'Eglise.** Turn right and follow the road into Les Houches, passing the church on your left, to arrive back at Les Houches Tourist Office.

1 (TP1) **Les Houches Tourist Office.** In front of you is the arch that marks the start and end of the TMB. It's a strangely emotional moment to complete your circuit of the trails around Mont Blanc, and to take a minute to think about what you've just achieved. You've circumnavigated the highest peak in the Alps, traversed three different countries and climbed more than 10,000m vertically. You've met people from many different countries around the world and stayed in a wide range of different mountain huts and villages. The kaleidoscope of memories and experiences will flicker before your eyes. It's amazing to watch different people's reactions at this moment. For some it's a huge achievement, and there are celebrations and tears of joy. For others, it's a moment of modest pride and reflection, and they sidle away to enjoy a quiet beer. Whatever the emotion, the TMB will live on inside you forever. Congratulations!

> **Chamonix** ⏺ While not strictly on the TMB route, the chances are that you'll get a transfer to and from Chamonix at either end of the TMB. It's often referred to as the Alpine capital, and certainly it's got a very good claim to that title. It's roughly three times as big as Courmayeur in terms of population and is far bigger than most first-time visitors expect. There is a vast array of shops in Chamonix, and if you are seeking any outdoor gear before the TMB, there are tens of stores to select from. It's also a good place to consider staying for a few extra days before or after your TMB, as there is such a great range of things to do in and around it.

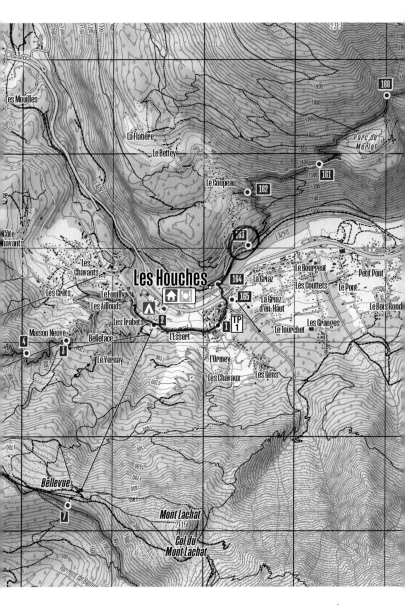

Les Moulles

La Flatière

Le Bettey

Parc de Merlet

160

Le Coupeau

162

161

163

L'Arve

Côte
havants

Les
Chavants

Le Bourgeat

Petit Pont

Les Couttets

Le Pont

164

La Griaz

Le Bois Rond

Les Houches

165

La Griaz
d'en-Haut

Les Crêts

Le Fouilly

Les Aillouds

Les Irabets

2

Les Granges

Le Tourchet

Maison Neuve

Belleface

L'Essert

L'Ormey

1

TP
1

4

3

Le Vernay

Les Chavaux

Les Gens

Bellevue

7

Mont Lachat
2115

Col du
Mont Lachat

2313

TOUR DU MONT BLANC
APPENDICES

Local information
Tourist Offices

Chamonix
85 Place du Triangle de l'Amitié,
74400 Chamonix-Mont-Blanc,
France
T +33 (0)4 50 53 00 24
www.chamonix.com

Les Houches
Place de la Mairie, BP 9,
74310 Les Houches,
France
T +33 (0)4 50 55 50 62
www.leshouches.com

Les Contamines-Montjoie
18 Route de Notre-Dame de la Gorge,
74170 Les Contamines-Montjoie,
France
T +33 (0)4 50 47 01 58
www.lescontamines.com

Courmayeur
CSC Centro Servizi, Viale Monte Bianco,
10, 11013 Courmayeur AO,
Italy
T +39 (0)165 842 060
www.lovevda.it/en

La Fouly
Route de Ferret 53, CH - 1944 La Fouly,
Switzerland
T +41 (0)27 775 23 84
www.lafouly.ch/en

Champex-Lac
Route du Lac 38, CH - 1938
Champex-Lac,
Switzerland
T +41 (0)27 775 23 83
www.champex.ch/en

Argentière
24 Route du Village, 74400 Argentière,
France
T +33 (0)4 50 54 02 14
www.argentiere-mont-blanc.com

Emergency services
France – 112
Italy – 112 or 118
Switzerland – 144

Mountain rescue
France – PGHM Chamonix
T +33 (0)4 50 53 16 89
France – PGHM Bourg-Saint-Maurice
T +33 (0)4 79 07 01 10
Italy – Val d'Aosta
T +39 (0)165 238 222
Switzerland – REGA 1414

Transport

Trains
www.sbb.ch/en/home.html
https://en.oui.sncf/en
www.seat61.com

Buses
www.gare-routiere.com
www.savda.it
www.sat-montblanc.com
www.ouibus.com

Minibus and taxi transfers
www.alpybus.com
www.mountaindropoffs.com
www.swiss-taxi.com/en
www.chamonix-valley-transfers.co.uk
www.taxifollonier.ch
www.taxi-montblanc.com/en

Passports and visas

www.ec.europa.eu/info/live-work-travel-eu_en

Languages

French, and to a lesser extent Italian, are the main languages spoken locally on the TMB; some basic English is widely spoken in accommodation on the trails and by people undertaking the route. Any attempt to communicate in the local language will always be appreciated.

Money and currency

The currency in France and Italy is euros; the currency in Switzerland is Swiss francs, but euros are generally accepted near the border. Note that most mountain huts do not accept credit cards so you will need to pay in cash.

ATMs are available in the following locations along and near the route:

- Chamonix
- Les Houches
- Les Contamines-Montjoie
- Courmayeur
- La Fouly
- Champex-Lac
- Argentière

Accommodation

Mountain huts, gîtes and hotels

Name	Closest timing point	Address	Website	Telephone	Email	Beds	Open
Chalet Les Méandres	1	1474, Montée de Coupeau, 74310 Les Houches, France	www.tupilak.com	+33 (0)4 50 54 56 66	emmanuel.ratouis@wanadoo.fr	24	All year
Chalet Hotel Les Campanules	1	450 Route de Coupeau, 74310 Les Houches, France	www.hotel-campanules.com	+33 (0)4 50 54 40 71	hotel-campanules@wanadoo.fr	100	All year
Hôtel Chris-Tal	1	242 Avenue des Alpages, 74310 Les Houches, France	www.chris-tal.com	+33 (0)4 50 54 50 55	info@chris-tal.com	50	All year
Hôtel Saint-Antoine	1	7 Route Napoléon, 74310 Les Houches, France	www.hotelsaintantoine.com	+33 (0)4 50 54 40 10	hotel-saint-antoine@wanadoo.fr	50	All year
Hôtel du Bois	1	475 Avenue des Alpages, 74310 Les Houches, France	www.hotel-du-bois.com	+33 (0)4 50 54 50 35	reservations@hotel-du-bois.com		All year
Gîte Michel Fagot	1	2 Allée des Sorbiers, 74310 Les Houches, France	www.gite-fagot.com	+33 (0)4 50 54 42 28	info@gite-fagot.com	36	All year
Hôtel Les Mélèzes	1	333 Rue de l'Essert, 74310 Les Houches, France	www.hotellesmelezes.com	+33 (0)4 50 54 40 09	hotel.lesmelezes@wanadoo.fr	100	All year
Auberge le Crêt	1	128 Route des Aillouds, 74310 Les Houches, France	https://auberge-le-cret.business.site	+33 (0)4 50 55 52 27		19	June to September
Hôtel Le Prarion	2	74170 St-Gervais Mont-Blanc, France	www.prarion.com	+33 (0)4 50 54 40 07	Yves@prarion.com	35	Mid-June to mid-September
Refuge du Fioux	2	4409 Route de Bionnassay, 74170 Saint-Gervais-les-Bains, France		+33 (0)4 50 93 52 43	serge.botholier@neuf.fr	24	June to September
Village APAS-BTP, Col de Voza	2	5274 Route de Bionnassay, 74170 Saint-Gervais-les-Bains, France	www.apas.asso.fr/vacances/col-de-voza-ete	+33 (0)4 50 54 79 43		150	All year
Auberge de Bionnassay	2	3084 Route de Bionnassay, 74170 Saint-Gervais-les-Bains, France	www.auberge-bionnassay.com	+33 (0)4 50 93 45 23	contact@auberge-bionnassay.com	38	June to September

Name	Closest timing point	Address	Website	Telephone	Email	Beds	Open
Refuge de Miage	3	1270 Route des Contamines, 74170 Saint-Gervais-les-Bains, France	www.refugedemiage.com	+33 (0)4 50 93 22 91 +33 (0)4 50 96 91 70 or +33 (0)6 31 72 50 19 (out of season)	refugedemiage@orange.fr	56	June to September
Auberge du Truc	3	64 Impasse des Creux, 74170 Les Contamines-Montjoie, France		+33 (0)4 50 93 12 48	aubergedutruc@hotmail.fr	28	Mid-June to mid-September
Hôtel La Clef des Champs	4	574 Route de la Frasse, 74170 Les Contamines-Montjoie, France	www.clefdeschampscontamines.wordpress.com	+33 (0)4 50 47 06 09	hotelclefdeschamps@free.fr	21	Mid-June to mid-September
Hôtel Gai Soleil	4	288 Chemin des Loyers, 74170 Les Contamines-Montjoie, France	www.gaisoleil.com	+33 (0)4 50 47 02 94	contact@gaisoleil.com	41	All year
Club Alpin Français Chalet des Contamines	4	22 Route du Plan du Moulin, 74170 Les Contamines-Montjoie, France	www.chaletdescontamines.ffcam.fr	+33 (0)4 50 47 00 88	chaletdescontamines@ffcam.fr	26	Mid-June to mid-September
Hôtel Le Christiania	4	593 Route de Notre-Dame de la Gorge, 74170 Les Contamines-Montjoie, France	www.lechristiania-hotel.com	+33 (0)4 50 47 02 72			All year
Gîte le Pontet	4	2485 Route de Notre-Dame de la Gorge, 74170 Les Contamines-Montjoie, France		+33 (0)4 50 47 04 04	campinglepontet74@orange.fr	61	June to September
Refuge de Nant Borrant	5	Chalet Refuge de Nant Borrant, 74170 Les Contamines-Montjoie, France	www.refuge-nantborrant.com	+33 (0)4 50 47 03 57	refugenantborrant@free.fr	35	June to September
Refuge de la Balme	6	Chemin du Col du Bonhomme, 74170 Les Contamines-Montjoie, France		+33 (0)4 50 47 03 54	refuge-labalme@outlook.fr	50	Mid-June to mid-September
Refuge du Col de la Croix du Bonhomme	7	Beaufortain, 73700 Bourg-Saint-Maurice, France	www.refugecroixdubonhomme.ffcam.fr	+33 (0)4 79 07 05 28	refugecroixdubonhomme@ffcam.fr	99	June to September
Les Chambres du Soleil	8	Les Chapieux, 73700 Bourg-Saint-Maurice, France	www.leschambresdusoleil-montblanc.com	+33 (0)4 79 31 30 22	lesoleildeschapieux@gmail.com	12	Mid-May to early October
Auberge de la Nova	8	Les Chapieux, 73700 Bourg-Saint-Maurice, France	www.refugelanova.com	+33 (0)9 82 12 64 35 +33 (0)6 64 94 98 35 (out of season)	info@refugelanova.com	65	Mid-May to early October
Refuge des Mottets	10	Vallée des Glaciers – Tour du Mont Blanc, 73700 Bourg-Saint-Maurice, France	www.lesmottets.com	+33 (0)4 79 07 01 70	refuge@lesmottets.com	80	June to September

Name	Closest timing point	Address	Website	Telephone	Email	Beds	Open
Rifugio Elisabetta Soldini	12	Lex Blanche Glacier Cap, 11013 Courmayeur, Italy	www.rifugioelisabetta.com	+39 (0)165 844 080	info@rifugioelisabetta.com	76	June to September
Cabane du Combal	13	Combal, Val Veny, 11013 Courmayeur, Italy	www.cabaneducombal.com	+39 (0)165 175 64 21	cabaneducombal@gmail.com	23	Mid-June to mid-September
Rifugio Maison Vieille	14	Col Checrouit, 11013 Courmayeur, Italy	www.maisonvieille.com	+39 (0)337 230 979 +39 (0)328 058 41 57	info@maisonvieille.com	45	Mid-June to September
Rifugio Le Randonneur	14	Prd Neyron Checrouit, 11013 Courmayeur, Italy	www.randonneurmb.com	+39 (0)349 536 88 98	info@randonneurmb.com	25	Mid-June to mid-September
Rifugio Monte Bianco	14	La Fodze, 11013 Courmayeur, Italy	www.rifugiomontebianco.com	+39 (0)165 869 097	info@rifugiomontebianco.com	70	June to September
La Casa per Ferie Notre Dame du Mont Blanc	15	Strada della Vittoria 24, Dolonne, 11013 Courmayeur, Italy	www.notredamedumontblanc.it	+39 (0)165 848 040	info@notredamedumontblanc.it	22	June to September
Hotel Lo Campagna	15	Rue des Granges 14, 11013 Courmayeur, Italy	www.locampagnar.it	+39 (0)165 844 154	info@locampagnar.it	25	All year
Hotel des Glaciers	15	Via della Vittoria 66, Dolonne, 11013 Courmayeur, Italy	www.hoteldesglaciers.com	+39 (0)165 842 037	info@hoteldesglaciers.com	40	All year
Hotel Dolonne	15	Via della Vittoria 62, Dolonne, 11013 Courmayeur, Italy	www.hoteldolonne.it	+39 (0)165 846 674	hoteldolonne@hoteldolonne.it	75	All year
Hotel De La Télécabine	15	Strada della Vittoria 28, Dolonne, 11013 Courmayeur, Italy	www.hoteldelatelecabine.com	+39 (0)165 846 767	hoteltelecabine@13maggio.com		All year
Hotel Stella del Nord	15	Strada della Vittoria 2, Dolonne, 11013 Courmayeur, Italy	www.stelladelnord.com	+39 (0)165 848 039	info@stelladelnord.com	25	All year
Hotel Ottoz	15	Strada Dolonne 9, 11013 Courmayeur, Italy	www.hotelottoz.net	+39 (0)165 846 681	info@hotelottoz.it	50	All year
Hotel Tavernier	15	Strada Courmayeur-Dolonne 27, 11013 Courmayeur, Italy	www.tavernier.it	+39 (0)165 841 080 +39 (0)11 859 175	tavernier@tin.it htavernier@virgilio.it		All year
Hotel Crampon	15	Strada la Villette 8, 11013 Courmayeur, Italy	www.crampon.it	+39 (0)165 842 385	info@crampon.it	50	All year

Name	Closest timing point	Address	Website	Telephone	Email	Beds	Open
Hotel Walser	15	Strada Margherita, 11013 Courmayeur, Italy	www.walserhotel.com	+39 (0)165 844 824 +39 (0)165 844 849	info@walserhotel.com	50	All year
Hotel Edelweiss	15	Via Marconi 42, 11013 Courmayeur, Italy	www.albergoedelweiss.it	+39 (0)165 841 590	info@albergoedelweiss.it	60	End of June to September
Hotel Svizzero	15	Strada Statale 26, n°11, 11013 Courmayeur, Italy	www.hotelsvizzero.com	+39 (0)165 848 170	info@hotelsvizzero.com	70	All year
Hotel Bouton d'Or	15	Strada Statale 26, n°10, 11013 Courmayeur, Italy	www.hotelboutondor.com	+39 (0)165 846 729	info@hotelboutondor.com	70	All year
Cresta Et Duc Hotel	15	Via Circonvallazione 7, 11013 Courmayeur, Italy		+39 (0)165 842 585		100	All year
Grand Hotel Royale Golf	15	Via Roma 87, 11013 Courmayeur, Italy	www.hotelroyalegolf.com	+39 (0)165 831 611	info@hotelroyalegolf.com	175	All year
Pensione Venezia	15	Strada la Villette 2, 11013 Courmayeur, Italy		+39 (0)165 842 461		25	All year
iH Hotels Courmayeur Mont Blanc Resort	15	Strada Statale 26, n°18, 11013 Courmayeur, Italy	www.ih-hotels.com/en/our-hotels/ih-hotels-courmayeur-mont-blanc-resort	+39 (0)165 846 555	frontoffice.montblanc@ih-hotels.com		All year
Hotel Croux	15	Via Croux 8, 11013 Courmayeur, Italy	www.hotelcroux.it	+39 (0)165 846 735	info@hotelcroux.it		All year
Hotel Lo Sciattolo	15	Viale Monte Bianco 50, 11013 Courmayeur, Italy	www.loscoiattolohotel.it	+39 (0)165 846 716	info@loscoiattolohotel.it		All year
Hotel Courmayeur	15	Via Roma 158, 11013 Courmayeur, Italy	www.hotelcourmayeur.it	+39 (0)165 846 732	info@hotelcourmayeur.com		All year
Hotel Cristallo	15	Via Roma 142, 11013 Courmayeur, Italy	www.hotelcristallocourmayeur.com	+39 (0)165 846 666	info@hotelcristallocourmayeur.com		All year
Le Vieux Pommier	15	Piazzale Monte Bianco 25, 11013 Courmayeur, Italy	www.levieuxpommier.it	+39 (0)165 842 281	info@levieuxpommier.it		All year
Petit Meublé	15	Strada Margherita 25, 11013 Courmayeur, Italy	www.petitmeublecourmayeur.com	+39 (0)165 842 426			All year
Hotel Meuble Laurent	15	Via Circonvallazione 23, 11013 Courmayeur, Italy		+39 (0)165 846 687		30	All year

Name	Closest timing point	Address	Website	Telephone	Email	Beds	Open
Maison Saint Jean	15	Vicolo Dolonne 18, 11013 Courmayeur, Italy	www.msj.it	+39 (0)165 842 880	info@msj.it	40	All year
Hotel Berthod	15	Via Mario Puchoz 11, 11013 Courmayeur, Italy	www.hotelberthod.com	+39 (0)165 842 835	info@hotelberthod.com	90	All year
Hotel Centrale	15	Via Mario Puchoz 7, 11013 Courmayeur, Italy	www.hotelcentralecourmayeur.com	+39 (0)165 846 644	info@hotelcentralecourmayeur.com	70	All year
Chalet Plan Goriet	15	Strada per Plan Gorret 45, 11013 Courmayeur, Italy	www.chaletplangorret.it	+39 (0)165 841 988	info@chaletplangorret.it	13	All year
Agriturismo Le Rêve	15	Rue Du Biolley 3, 11013 Courmayeur, Italy	www.agriturismolereve.com	+39 (0)165 842 861	agrilereve@gmail.com	16	All year
Hotel del Viale	15	Viale Monte Bianco 74, 11013 Courmayeur, Italy	www.hoteldelviale.com	+39 (0)165 846 712	info@hoteldelviale.com		All year
Villa Novecento	15	Viale Monte Bianco 64, 11013 Courmayeur, Italy	www.villanovecento.it	+39 (0)165 182 56 22			All year
Grand Hotel Courmayeur Mont Blanc	15	Strada Grand Ru 1, 11013 Courmayeur, Italy	www.grandhotelcourmayeurmontblanc.it	+39 (0)165 844 542	info@hcmontblanc.it		All year
Gran Baita Hotel & Wellness	15	Strada Larzey 2, 11013 Courmayeur, Italy	www.hotelgranbaita.it	+39 (0)165 844 040	granbaita@alpissima.it		All year
La Maison du Meuny	15	Via Col Ferret 29, La Saxe, 11013 Courmayeur, Italy	www.maisondemeuny.it	+39 (0)349 604 47 24 +39 (0)333 464 94 86	maisondemeuny@gmail.com		All year
L'Abri des Amis	15	Strada Entrelevie SA, 11013 Courmayeur, Italy	www.labridesamis.it	+39 (0)349 815 54 04	info@labridesamis.it	19	June to September
Albergo dei Camosci	15	Strada per Entrèves 7, 11013 Courmayeur, Italy	www.hoteldeicamosci.com	+39 (0)165 842 338	info@hoteldeicamosci.com		All year
Maison La Saxe	15	Via Cardinale Berthod, 22, 11013 Courmayeur, Italy	www.maisonlasaxe.it	+39 (0)344 117 55 30	info@maisonlasaxe.it	12	All year
Rifugio Bertone	17	Monte de la Saxe, 11013 Courmayeur, Italy	www.rifugiobertone.it	+39 (0)347 032 57 85	info@rifugiobertone.it	60	June to September
Hotel Lavachey	19	Val Ferret 1, Fraz. Lavachey, 11013 Courmayeur, Italy	www.lavachey.com	+39 (0)165 869 723	info@lavachey.com	25	Mid-June to September

Name	Closest timing point	Address	Website	Telephone	Email	Beds	Open
Rifugio Bonatti	19	11013 Courmayeur, Italy	*www.rifugiobonatti.it*	+39 (0)335 684 85 78	info@rifugiobonatti.com	80	June to September
Chalet Val Ferret	20	Arnouva 1, Val Ferret, 11013 Courmayeur, Italy	*www.chaletvalferret.com*	+39 (0)165 844 959	info@chaletvalferret.com	21	Mid-June to mid-September
Rifugio Elena	21	Fraz. Lavachey, 11013 Courmayeur, Italy	*www.rifugioelena.it*	+39 (0)165 844 688	info@rifugioelena.it	127	Mid-June to mid-September
Gîte Alpage de la Peule	22	Somlaprez 35, 1937 Orsières, Switzerland		+41 (0)27 783 10 41 +41 (0)27 783 32 70 (out of season)	nicolas.lapeule@gmail.com	33	Mid-June to mid-September
Hotel du Col de Fenêtre	23	Ferret 6, 1944 La Fouly, Switzerland	*https://hotelducoldefenetre.business.site*	+41 (0)27 783 11 88	hotelducoldefenetre@gmail.com	37	Mid-June to mid-September
Gîte de la Léchère	23	Dessous 2, 1944 La Fouly, Switzerland	*www.lalechere.ch*	+41 (0)27 783 30 64	chloe.sarrasin29@hotmail.com	35	June to September
Maya-Joie	24	Route du Barfay 4, 1944 La Fouly, Switzerland	*www.mayajoie.ch*	+41 (0)27 565 56 30	contact@mayajoie.ch	45	May to October
Auberge des Glaciers	24	1944 La Fouly, Switzerland	*www.aubergedesglaciers.ch*	+41 (0)27 783 11 71	info@aubergedesglaciers.ch	56	June to September
Chalet Le Dolent	24	Route du Barfay 6, 1944 La Fouly, Switzerland	*www.dolent.ch*	+41 (0)79 220 39 91	info@dolent.ch	30	All year
Grand Hotel La Fouly	24	1944 La Fouly, Switzerland	*www.grandhotellafouly.ch*	+41 (0)27 783 11 77	info@grandhotellafouly.ch	129	All year
L'Edelweiss	24	Route de Ferret 44, 1944 La Fouly, Switzerland	*www.fouly.ch*	+41 (0)27 783 26 21	info@fouly.ch		All year
Croquenature	25	Chantal Maudry, les Arlaches 9, 1943 Praz-de-Fort, Switzerland	*www.croquenature.ch*	+41 (0)79 509 14 24		7	All year
Hotel Belvédère	26	Route du Signal, 1938 Orsières, Switzerland		+41 (0)27 783 11 14		18	All year
Hotel Alpina	26	Route du Signal 32, 1938 Orsières, Switzerland	*www.alpinachampex.ch*	+41 (0)27 783 18 92	t.ssieres@romandie.com		All year

Name	Closest timing point	Address	Website	Telephone	Email	Beds	Open
Hotel Splendide	26	Famille Richer-Lonfat, 1938 Champex-Lac, Switzerland	www.hotel-splendide.ch	+41 (0)27 783 11 45	hotel-splendide@bluemail.ch	15	All year
Hotel Mont Lac	26	Route du Lac 6, 1938 Champex-Lac, Switzerland	www.hotel-montlac.com	+41 (0)26 565 66 00	hotelmontlac@gmail.com		All year
Ptarmigan	26	Route du Lac 14, 1938 Champex-Lac, Switzerland	www.ptarmigan.ch	+41 (0)27 783 16 40 +41 (0)78 766 85 36		6	All year
Le Cabanon	26	Route du Lac 3, 1938 Champex-Lac, Switzerland	www.le-cabanon.ch	+41 (0)27 783 11 72	info@le-cabanon.ch	8	All year
Chalet du Jardin Alpin	26	Flore-Alpe, Route de l'Adray 27, 1938 Champex-Lac, Switzerland	www.flore-alpe.ch	+41 (0)27 783 12 17	reservation@flore-alpe.ch	16	May to mid-October
Pension en Plein Air	26	Route du Lac 45, 1938 Champex-Lac, Switzerland	www.pensionenpleinair.ch/pensionen	+41 (0)27 783 23 50	pensionenpleinair@gmail.com	62	Mid-June to mid-September
Hotel du Glacier	26	Famille Biselx, 1938 Champex-Lac, Switzerland	www.hotelglacier.ch	+41 (0)27 782 61 51	info@hotelglacier.ch		All year
Au Club Alpin	26	Route du Lac, 1938 Champex-Lac, Switzerland	www.auclubalpin.ch				All year
Au Vieux Champex	26	1938 Champex-Lac, Switzerland		+41 (0)27 783 12 16			All year
Les Marmottes Bed and Breakfast	26	Chemin du Fratsoy 6, 1938 Champex-Lac, Switzerland		+41 (0)78 759 64 29			All year
Boulangerie Gentiana, Champex	26	Route du Lac 35, 1938 Champex-Lac, Switzerland		+41 (0)27 783 12 58			All year
Relais d'Arpette	26	1938 Champex-Lac, Switzerland	www.arpette.ch	+41 (0)27 783 12 21	info@arpette.ch	100	June to September
La Grange	26	Route du Vallon 10, 1938 Champex-Lac, Switzerland	www.lagrangechampex.com	+41 (0)79 948 75 76	info@lagrangechampex.com	12	June to September
Gîte Bon Abri	26	Route du Vallon 9, 1938 Champex-Lac, Switzerland	www.gite-bon-abri.com	+41 (0)27 783 14 23	contact@gite-bon-abri.com	54	June to September
Hotel Sunways	26	1938 Champex-Lac, Switzerland	www.sunways.ch	+41 (0)27 783 11 22	hotel@sunways.ch		All year

Name	Closest timing point	Address	Website	Telephone	Email	Beds	Open
Hôtel du Col de la Forclaz	28	Famille JC Gay-Crosier, 1929 Trient, Switzerland	www.coldelaforclaz.ch	+41 (0)27 722 26 88	colforclazhotel@bluewin.ch	65	January to mid-November
Auberge du Mont-Blanc	28	1929 Trient, Switzerland	www.aubergemontblanc.com	+41 (0)27 767 15 05	info@aubergemontblanc.com	120	June to September
Hôtel La Grande Ourse	28	Le Betty 30, 1929 Trient, Switzerland	www.la-grande-ourse.ch	+41 (0)27 722 17 54	contact@la-grande-ourse.ch	80	June to September
Refuge Le Peuty	28	Le Peuty 32, 1929 Trient, Switzerland	www.refugelepeuty.ch	+41 (0)78 719 29 83	info@refugelepeuty.ch	22	June to September
Refuge Les Grands	29	1929 Trient, Switzerland		+41 (0)79 928 65 38	nic@azymuthe.ch		All year
Gîte d'Alpage Les Ecuries de Charamillon	29	Charamillon mountain pastures , Le Tour, 74400 Chamonix Mont Blanc, France	www.les-ecuries-de-charamillon.fr	+33 (0)4 50 54 17 07 +33 (0)6 70 12 85 04 (out of season)		19	Mid-June to mid-September
Refuge du Col de Balme	29	Le Tour, 74400 Chamonix Mont Blanc, France		+33 (0)6 07 06 16 30	henri.lapeyrere@gmail.com	20	Mid-June to mid-September
Hôtel Restaurant L'Olympique	30	Place du Tour 230, 74400 Chamonix Mont Blanc, France	www.hotel-olympique-chamonix.com	+33 (0)4 50 54 01 04	hotel.olympique@orange.fr		All year
Auberge La Boerne	30	288 Chemin de Trélechamps, Argentière, 74400 Chamonix Mont Blanc, France	www.la-boerne.fr	+33 (0)4 50 54 05 14	contact@la-boerne.fr	31	All year
Gîte Le Moulin	30	32 Chemin du Moulin des Frasserands, Argentière, 74400 Chamonix Mont Blanc, France	www.gite-chamonix.com	+33 (0)6 82 33 34 54	benoit.henry2@wanadoo.fr	38	All year
Chalet Alpin du Tour	30	Chemin du Rocher Nay, Le Tour, 74400 Chamonix Mont Blanc, France	www.chaletdutour.ffcam.fr	+33 (0)4 50 54 04 16		78	April to mid-September
Refuge du Lac Blanc	31	Les Alpages des Chéserys, 74400 Chamonix Mont Blanc, France	www.refuge-lac-blanc.fr	+33 (0)7 67 56 74 14	contactaurefugedulacblanc@gmail.com	40	Mid-June to end of September
Refuge de la Flégère	32	74400 Chamonix Mont Blanc, France		+33 (0)6 03 58 28 14			All year
Refuge de Bellachat	34	305 Route de vers le Nant, 74400 Chamonix Mont Blanc, France	www.refuge-bellachat.com	+33 (0)7 89 03 30 38	refuge.bellachat@gmail.com	24	End of June to mid-September

Campsites

Name	Closest timing point	Address	Website	Telephone	Email	Open
Camping Bellevue	1	136 Route du Nant Jorland, 74310 Les Houches, France		+33 (0)6 33 50 34 12	serge.botholier@neuf.fr	June to September
Refuge du Fioux	2	4409 Route de Bionnassay, 74170 Saint-Gervais-les-Bains, France		+33 (0)4 50 93 52 43		June to September
Refuge de Miage	3	1270 Route des Contamines, 74170 Saint-Gervais-les-Bains, France	www.refugedemiage.com	+33 (0)4 50 93 22 91 +33 (0)4 50 96 91 70 or +33 (0)6 31 72 50 19 (out of season)	refugedemiage@orange.fr	June to September
Camping le Pontet	4	2485 Route de Notre Dame de la Gorge, 74170 Les Contamines-Montjoie, France	www.campinglepontet.fr	+33 (0)4 50 47 04 04	campinglepontet74@orange.fr	June to September
Aire de Bivouac La Rollaz	5	74170 Les Contamines-Montjoie, France				
Aire de Bivouac de la Balme	6	74170 Les Contamines-Montjoie, France				
Refuge de la Balme	6	Chemin du Col du Bonhomme, 74170 Les Contamines-Montjoie, France		+33 (0)4 50 47 03 54	refuge-labalme@outlook.fr	Mid-June to mid-September
Refuge du Col de la Croix du Bonhomme	7	Beaufortain, 73700 Bourg-Saint-Maurice, France	www.refugecroixdubonhomme.ffcam.fr	+33 (0)4 79 07 05 28	refugecroixdubonhomme@ffcam.fr	June to September
Les Chapieux*	8	Les Chapieux, 73700 Bourg-Saint-Maurice, France				
Camping Monte Bianco La Sorgente**	14	Peuterey, Val Veny, 11013 Courmayeur, Italy	www.campinglasorgente.net	+39 (0)389 90 20 772	info@campinglasorgente.net	
Camping Aiguille Noire**	14	La Zerotta Val Veny, 11013 Courmayeur, Italy	www.aiguillenoire.com	+39 (0)347 54 77 941	info@aiguillenoire.com	From May
Hobo Camping**	14	Cuignon 7, Val Veny, 11013 Courmayeur, Italy	www.campinghobo.com	+39 (0)165 86 90 73	info@campinghobo.com	June to August
Camping Grandes Jorasses***	17	Via per la Val Ferret 53, 11013 Courmayeur, Italy	www.grandesjorasses.com	+39 (0)165 869 708	info@grandesjorasses.com	

Name	Closest timing point	Address	Website	Telephone	Email	Open
Camping Tronchey***	19	Tronchey, Val Ferret, 11013 Courmayeur, Italy	www.tronchey.com	+39 (0)165 869 707	info@tronchey.com	Mid-June to mid-September
Camping des Glaciers	24	Chemin de Tsamodet 36, 1944 La Fouly, Switzerland	www.camping-glaciers.ch	+41 (0)27 783 18 26	info@camping-glaciers.ch	May to early October
Relais d'Arpette	26	1938 Champex-Lac, Switzerland	www.arpette.ch	+41 (0)27 783 12 21	info@arpette.ch	June to September
Gîte Bon Abri	26	Route du Valon 9, 1938 Champex-Lac, Switzerland	www.gite-bon-abri.com	+41 (0)27 783 14 23	contact@gite-bon-abri.com	June to September
Camping Les Rocailles	26	Route de Champex, 1938 Champex-Lac, Switzerland	www.champex-camping.ch	+41 (0)27 783 19 79		
Camping de la Forclaz	28	Famille JC Gay-Crosier, 1929 Trient, Switzerland	www.coldelaforclaz.ch	+41 (0)27 722 26 88	colforclazhotel@bluewin.ch	
Le Peuty	28	Le Peuty, 1929 Trient, Switzerland				
Aiguilles Rouges Nature Reserve****	30	Maison de Village, 74400 Argentière, France	www.reserves-aiguilles-rouges.com/english.html			
Chalets Pierre Semard	30	400 Chemin des Frasserands, 74400 Chamonix-Mont-Blanc, France		+33 (0)4 50 54 00 29		

* Camping is permitted in the wildflower meadow close to Auberge de la Nova.

** Off route, in Val Veny.

*** On Variation 4.

**** Camping is generally not permitted in France's nature reserves, but you are permitted to bivouac for one night between 7 p.m. and 9 a.m. (see website for details).

About the author

Kingsley Jones is a UIMLA International Mountain Leader, who has guided trekking and running groups on the Tour du Mont Blanc well over 50 times, and has raced it multiple times in the Ultra-Trail du Mont Blanc (UTMB) running event. Put in context, he's spent well over a year of his life on the trails of the Tour du Mont Blanc, so knows every step of it. Kingsley divides his time between the Alps and the English Lake District; when not guiding for his company Icicle, he's a mountain rescue volunteer in the Lake District. His personal climbing achievements include all six classic north faces of the Alps, and numerous expeditions around the world. He is an award-winning outdoor writer, having previously published *Trail Running – Chamonix and the Mont Blanc Region* and *Trail and Fell Running in the Lake District*.

www.kingsleyjones.com
www.icicle.co.uk

Vertebrate Publishing

At Vertebrate Publishing we publish books to inspire adventure.

It's our rule that the only books we publish are those that we'd want to read or use ourselves. We endeavour to bring you beautiful books that stand the test of time and that you'll be proud to have on your bookshelf for years to come.

The Peak District was the inspiration behind our first books. Our offices are situated on its doorstep, minutes away from world-class climbing, biking and hillwalking. We're driven by our own passion for the outdoors, for exploration, and for the natural world; it's this passion that we want to share with our readers.

We aim to inspire everyone to get out there. We want to connect readers – young and old – with the outdoors and the positive impact it can have on well-being. We think it's particularly important that young people get outside and explore the natural world, something we support through our publishing programme.

As well as publishing award-winning new books, we're working to make available many out-of-print classics in both print and digital formats. These are stories that we believe are unique and significant; we want to make sure that they continue to be shared and enjoyed.

www.v-publishing.co.uk

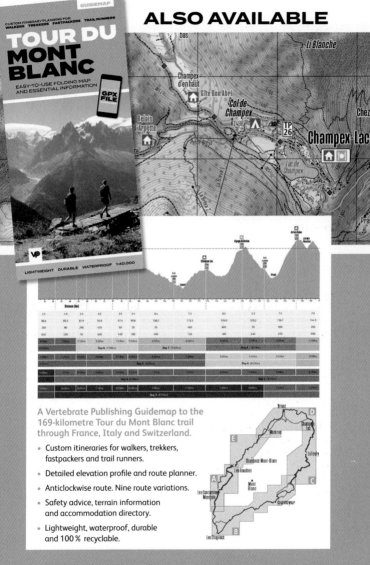
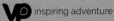

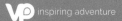